THE RESPONSIVE CITY

Engaging Communities Through Data-Smart Governance

Stephen Goldsmith
Susan Crawford

JB JOSSEY-BASS™

A Wiley Brand

Published by Jossey-Bass
A Wiley Brand
One Montgomery Street, Suite 1200, San Francisco, CA 94104-4594
www.josseybass.com

Jossey-Bass books and products are available through most bookstores. To contact Jossey-Bass directly call our Customer Care Department within the U.S. at 800-956-7739, outside the U.S. at 317-572-3986, or fax 317-572-4002.

Wiley publishes in a variety of print and electronic formats and by print-on-demand. Some material included with standard print versions of this book may not be included in e-books or in print-on-demand. If this book refers to media such as a CD or DVD that is not included in the version you purchased, you may download this material at http://booksupport.wiley.com. For more information about Wiley products, visit www.wiley.com.

Library of Congress Cataloging-in-Publication Data
Goldsmith, Stephen, 1946-
  The responsive city : engaging communities through data-smart governance / Stephen Goldsmith and Susan Crawford.
    pages com
  Includes bibliographical references and index.
  ISBN 978-1-118-91090-0 (hardback); ISBN 978-1-118-91121-1 (pdf); ISBN 978-1-118-91093-1 (epub)
  1. Internet in public administration—United States. 2. Public-private sector cooperation—United States. 3. Cities and town—United States. 4. Digital media—United States I. Crawford, Susan, 1963-II. Title.
  JK468.A8G63 2014
  352.3′821602854678—dc23

                                                                                    2014019126

Printed in the United States of America
FIRST EDITION
HB Printing 10 9 8 7 6 5 4 3

Contents

Foreword

There is no better way to improve the lives of billions of people around the world than to improve the way cities work. For the first time in human history, the majority of the world's people live in cities. By 2050, 75 percent will. As more and more people move to cities, more and more of the world's challenges—and solutions—will be concentrated there, too.

The rise of cities coincides with a technological revolution that is empowering local leaders to find innovative new ways to better serve the public. At the center of that revolution is our growing ability to use data to improve the services that government provides. Governments have long been in the business of keeping records, and increasingly they are using those records—billions of data points—to improve everything from emergency response to education to transportation.

I have a rule of thumb: if you can't measure it, you can't manage it. And I brought that approach with me from the private sector to New York's city hall. Our administration looked for ways to use data—and to collect more data—to help us better serve New Yorkers.

In 2003, we launched 311, a nonemergency government information and services hotline available to New Yorkers twenty-four hours a day, seven days a week. Not only did 311 make it easier for New Yorkers to get information from the city—and to file complaints—it also gave city government more information on what New Yorkers were concerned about and helped us keep track of how well we were doing at addressing those concerns.

We also created data systems to measure agency performance and hold ourselves accountable for results. And we took a page from the private sector and brought predictive analytics to local government, using city data to help foresee the challenges of the future—and took action to address them today.

Harnessing and understanding data helped us decide how to allocate resources more efficiently and effectively, which allowed us to improve the delivery of services—from protecting children and fighting crime to repairing potholes and inspecting buildings—while also saving taxpayer money.

Cities and mayors everywhere are recognizing the powerful role data can play in bringing more transparency, accountability, and efficiency to government—and Bloomberg Philanthropies is helping to support this work. For instance, in 2013 the city of Chicago was one of five winners of the Mayors Challenge, an ideas competition for cities, for its groundbreaking idea to use data to help city government prevent problems before they develop. Chicago is quickly setting a new standard, which other cities will surely follow.

Across so much of the work we do with cities—from our innovation delivery program helping New Orleans reduce gun violence to our work with cities around the world to reduce carbon emissions—we see data enabling new and creative approaches. Of course, driving change in cities requires more than just data. It also requires strong managers and creative problem solvers—and Stephen Goldsmith is both. I was lucky to have him join me at city hall as a deputy mayor during my third term in office, and he helped us take our efforts to improve city services to new levels.

In the chapters that follow, Goldsmith and his talented coauthor, Susan Crawford, demonstrate how local leaders are changing the way governments work. Through case studies from New York City, Boston, and Chicago, they explain how data mining, empowered public servants, mobile apps, wireless devices, technically supported citizens, and social media can produce a dramatically more responsive city. And they show how these tools can be used by both elected and community leaders to drive change and improve a neighborhood's quality of life.

Cities will increasingly define the future, in America and around the world. And cities that capitalize on the technology revolution will lead the way. This book helps point the way forward.

June 2014   Michael Bloomberg
                                    Former mayor of New York City

Introduction

Urban government in the United States today is at a critical juncture. Never before over the last century has there been such a need to change the way city hall works. And never has there been such an opportunity to do it. The century-old framework of local government—centralized, compartmentalized bureaucracies that jealously guard information and adhere to strict work rules—is frustrating and disappointing its constituents, whose trust in government is at an all-time low. Residents in many cities despair of getting the services they need from city hall, especially in places where financial stresses are making governments even less responsive than in the past. Yet local government has the means to completely reverse this trend toward despair. That opportunity comes from digital technology: new ways of gathering, storing, and analyzing data; new modes of communication; and the new world of social networks. With these digital tools, citizens and their officials can revolutionize local government, making it more responsive, transparent, and cost-effective than it has ever been.

A confluence of technology advancements now promises broad and constructive change in local government, altering everything from the way workers perform basic functions to the way citizens engage with government. Social media and data science are spurring a sense of renewed civic engagement, which will cause broad changes in government.

This book is about that revolution and the people who are leading it. Specifically, it is about the insights and skills they are applying to digital governance and the institutional obstacles that they have overcome. In the chapters that follow, you will see precisely how data-smart, responsive governance has paid off in

1

a variety of cities, and you will see how the pioneers whose stories we present achieved that payoff.

One of us (Goldsmith) has worked for decades in and for cities—as a community volunteer, prosecutor, mayor, deputy mayor, and federal official involved with service to cities. The other (Crawford) has been involved in technology policy as a Washington lawyer, White House advisor, and law professor. In our careers, we have watched American cities face countless challenges, from riots to staff layoffs to bankruptcy. We have also seen cities experience a renaissance in safety, economic growth, and livability. Consistently, though, through good times and bad, there has been a steady rise in residents' complaints about uncaring bureaucrats and unresponsive city halls.

We know that cities can do better. We both teach graduate students at Harvard University who have grown up in the digital era: Goldsmith as the director of the Innovations in Government program at Harvard Kennedy School and Crawford as a codirector of Harvard's Berkman Center for Internet and Society. We and our students see the great opportunities digital technology offers local government. Harvard's Data-Smart City Solutions initiative, funded by grants from Bloomberg Philanthropies, the John D. and Catherine T. MacArthur Foundation, and the John S. and James L. Knight Foundation, features the accomplishments of public and civic leaders who use data to produce effective governance. We hope, through this book and our ongoing work, to help those digital possibilities become reality.

Though we discuss technology throughout this book, technology is not our main subject. Rather, this is a book about the leaders—public, nonprofit, and community—who have forced changes in the status quo by capitalizing on the power of the new tools.

We know the digital age that has so changed every aspect of life can also fundamentally improve local government and raise the civic spirit of our people and the officials who serve them. But experience has shown us that this great advance cannot begin without major changes in governance: bureaucratic structures must be upgraded to accommodate the new technologies and their uses. As the digital city hall replaces one based on paper, cities will have to jettison the structures of governance that have served them for more than a hundred years.

In the past century, when the flow of information was slower and more limited, the best government could do to keep control and ensure quality was to define rules and enforce adherence to them. Today, with data flowing freely among employees and citizens, that rule-bound approach is an obstacle to effective action. City employees can act more quickly and creatively to resolve issues when their jobs are defined as problem solving rather than rule following. Instead of filing reports and waiting for overburdened supervisors to respond, workers can make their own decisions, aided by curated and organized data, and supported often by real-time advice from managers. The result is a smarter and nimbler government that better employs its resources and attention.

Some of the components of city hall's digital revolution are familiar from daily life. There are smartphones and tablets, which move data from file cabinets in city hall to workers out in the field—and in turn let those workers send back new information as soon as they have it. Apps enabled by global positioning systems (GPS) can reveal where employees are performing their work and how long discrete tasks take. That makes it possible to detect unusually good (or unusually bad) performance by an employee and send a notice to a supervisor in real time. Other key digital tools come from private enterprise: methods for storing, organizing, visualizing, and curating data to generate reliable insights and fast responses. These tools allow community groups and government officials alike to make discoveries about their neighborhoods that would elude even the sharpest analysis from the most highly trained specialist.

These discoveries are possible because the digital revolution encompasses more than how data is handled. It's also a radical expansion of the sources of information. To data that comes from government's usual methods—potholes reported, streets plowed, hours spent per complaint—residents themselves can now add massive amounts of information that governments could not, or would not, collect in earlier times. Anonymized data from E-ZPass readers or sensors in the street can reveal patterns in traffic or in the use of city resources. Twitter, Facebook, and other social media create a 24/7 window into what people are noticing, celebrating, or decrying. This combination of self-generated "big data" about people's behavior and their own contributions to social media is a rich vein of information about almost any problem a city government confronts. Of course, public servants themselves also generate such data, which they can now share easily with one another and with nonprofit organizations, community groups, media, and private companies. Only a decade ago, the 311 call center, that central always-on clearinghouse where citizens can phone in their requests for service and information, represented a major advance over the limitations of a fragmented government bureaucracy. Today the 311 center looks obsolete. The twenty-first century's equivalent of 311 won't be confined to phones or to service requests and questions. Instead, it will be a platform for citizens to engage city hall, and each other, through text, voice, social media, and other apps.

This book focuses on the emerging cadre of officials and civic activists who are using the new data tools to transform city government. We tell their stories, describing the transformations they have already managed to achieve. We also highlight the drivers of that transformation—organizational change to remove hierarchies and bureaucracies; the sharing of data in forms that make it understandable and useful to people in government and outside it; and, perhaps most important, leadership.

Leadership is essential because the new type of public servant we describe must break down three barriers to progress that business-as-usual bureaucratic government imposes. First, there is a narrow and technical definition of what constitutes good work by government employees; second, the vertical silos of the usual city government's organization block the free flows of ideas and information, making it ill suited to problems that don't fit into the "verticals"; and, third, the bureaucracy orients itself to performing and measuring activities (potholes filled, cases processed) rather than solutions to problems. To benefit from digital technology, in other words, government must get out of its own way. That requires that it set aside some of the structures, traditions, and habits that have accumulated over the past 125 years.

Reformers brought about those structures in response to the chaotic free-for-all that characterized city government in the nineteenth century. Eager to rid themselves of corruption, incompetence, and unreliability in city hall, Progressive reformers in the late 1800s enshrined rationality, professional standards, and the division of labor. Government was centralized and organized into separate functional areas (firefighters for fires, public health nurses for epidemics, trash collectors for sanitation). Workers were chosen for meeting clear standards rather than for their political connections, and they were given well-defined tasks and assessed on their performance. Managers told employees what to do; employees reported back to managers in a clear chain of command.

Clearly defined tasks were a crucial feature of the reforms of the nineteenth-century Progressives. And so government was focused on producing activities rather than solutions. Officials measured how many homeless beds, how much health care, how many potholes filled rather than actual reductions in homelessness, improvements in health and education, and the overall smoothness of the streets. Government was securely protected against any abuse of discretion through an orientation toward compliance with regulations, not toward results. While serving as chairman of the board of the Corporation for National and Community Service (the federal parent of AmericaCorps VISTA, Senior Corps, and many faith initiatives) one of us (Goldsmith) saw the unfortunate consequences of this orientation. If a nonprofit produced terrific results but did not keep its books correctly, it was harshly penalized and considered a failure. If an organization accomplished nothing but did so with impeccable bookkeeping, the corporation's inspectors judged it successful.

And so we arrive at the crisis that city government faces today. Structures that produced progressive government in 1890 ensure regressive results in 2014. Public officials work in narrow spaces confined by civil service laws, labor contracts, job classifications, court cases, and risk-averse lawyers. Layers of bureaucracy, inflexible rule applications, redundant multiple agency involvement in a single transaction, and tone deafness to citizens became the hallmarks of government as progressive government overgrew itself. Again and again, local and state officials, hemmed in by federal mandates, miss commonsense breakthroughs because of the way they are organized and regulated. Confined to verticals, with a different agency responsible for each program, public servants strain to engage with constituents who, like all other people, live their lives "horizontally"—in neighborhoods and families, not within the purview of the sanitation department or the housing agency.

Not only did complexity and rule-driven accountability affect the way we manufactured government; it also affected the way government regulated. As the twentieth century advanced, this system broke down. Problems spread across the neat organizational lines that divided building inspection from health from fire. Citizens who were used to smartphone apps lost their patience when told they had to wait for documents to be found in file cabinets and put in the mail. Local governments addressed risk in a complex society by imposing more regulations. When serious breakdowns occurred, watchdogs and monitoring procedures also were piled on. To deal with problems that didn't fit neatly into departmental divisions, working groups were fastened onto the older bureaucratic structures. Meanwhile, even while stretching to do its old job, local government added new responsibilities to its portfolio. The federal government led this charge with a vast array of regulations and programs it imposed on cities and states. Courts also handed down mandates. City hall, once concerned with fires, crimes, sanitation, and other basic services, now expands its reach from prenatal to preschool through to senior services and scores of services in between. The expansion of services coupled with the increasing complexity of modern life made government workers' jobs more difficult to break down into clear, simple, easily supervised tasks.

We need a postprogressive response by government, and this century's digital tools are perfectly equipped to sweep these frustrations away.[1] Because they can collect, analyze, and share information so efficiently, these technologies push both government and its constituents to focus on results rather than compliance. This frees up the talents and judgment of government workers, letting them spend more time solving problems and less time proving they adhered to rigid standards. Moreover, that ability to share data undermines the vertical organization of traditional government, encouraging horizontal exchanges among departments (and, of course, among community groups and other stakeholders outside city hall). This can open up the machinery of government to its people, letting them collaborate to create solutions coproduced by public servants and their constituents. In the place of bureaucratic and centralized structures that frustrate citizens and officials alike, information technology can deliver government whenever and however citizens need it. The result is a smarter and nimbler government that better deploys its resources and attention.

Refreshingly, we also see that a citizen's judgment concerning the trustworthiness of the local government can be facilitated by public transparency and social media use, resulting in more participation in solving the community's problems. This social-media-engendered trust can produce an enhanced role in areas from policy to development to planning. We can see from international research work that "although social media cannot promise to unite both institutions and citizens one hundred percent, to a certain extent, it can facilitate effectiveness in two important perspectives: (1) build social capital via online civic engagement and (2) instill a sense of confidence and trust in the government and justice system."[2]

In this book, we present stories of digital efforts designed to accomplish just this kind of trust building. More important, we describe the successful struggles of people who managed to overcome resistance to change.

Saving Children with Tablets

For twenty years Jim Payne presided over Juvenile Court in Marion County, Indiana. Each year he and his magistrates adjudicated over twelve thousand delinquency cases that had been investigated by police officers assigned to their department's juvenile branch, prepared for court and sentencing by the juvenile probation department, and filed by a separate prosecutor's office. Payne's courts also handled matters involving more than one thousand neglected and abused children annually, whose cases were investigated by workers from the county welfare department. Some of the neglect cases also involved school social workers who had identified young children who had frequently missed school. That adds up to five different departments addressing the same problem but never sharing information.

Payne tried for years to get these five departments to pool, or at least share, their data. His first opponents were lawyers for each administrative unit, who explained that even if information sharing would help children, it could not be done. Payne fought and won that legal battle, but it had little immediate practical effect a decade ago when his victory occurred. The data that could now be shared existed only on paper. As long as data could move only by briefcase and envelope, there would be no free flow of collaborative information in real time.

When Payne moved on to become director of the Indiana State Department of Child Services, he continued to press for shared data, but the situation in his new job was no better than the one he had left. His caseworkers took their notepads into challenging homes without access to relevant records from schools, family doctors, mental health providers, the criminal justice system, or other sources. Payne had inherited a statewide information system, required of Indiana and other states by federal government standards, that was designed for data storage and control, not getting information to employees who were trying to help troubled children.

With the assistance of the Annie E. Casey Foundation, Payne addressed this problem by launching the country's leading effort to eliminate paper in child welfare services, adopt digital processes, and get digital tools to the field. The department's data services were redesigned so that information could be gathered and carefully shared with those with a need and legal right to know, including foster parents, education professionals, medical staff, and service providers. Data from other departments (e.g., Corrections and Family and Social Services) was integrated and also made accessible pursuant to a set of rules that allowed the information to be used by the child service employees involved with the family. Payne's department purchased laptops and tablets for every caseworker, allowing them to add information to a case file in real time and giving them the ability to get the information they needed exactly when they needed it. The goal, of course, was to equip fieldworkers facing time-sensitive critical questions with far more information to make decisions. Indiana's efforts against the abuse of children are no longer just run on the hunches of young caseworkers; they are now fought with intuition and discretion informed by hard information and performance metrics.

Payne has found that the ability to look peripherally, that is, to see across the verticals of many agencies and systems, is essential to making best decisions for the safety and well-being of children. His reforms aimed to create such peripheral vision, and in doing so they have produced demonstrably better outcomes. The effort had the additional virtue of spreading beyond Payne's department to improve the workings of other parts of Indiana's state government. The state's chief information officer under Governor Mike Pence, Paul Baltzell, decided to leverage data even more to take on infant mortality, which we will explore further in the final chapter.

Coordinated, Precision Crime Fighting

In November 2011, Mayor Michael Bloomberg of New York City appointed Shari Hyman commissioner of the city's Business Integrity Commission (BIC). Hyman had served in several jobs that helped her understand how a government's propensity to treat all incidents identically reduces its effectiveness against the real "bad guys" even as it creates substantial red tape and increases costs for honest small businesspeople. As director of business acceleration, she focused on streamlining city operations to help small businesses. For instance, she designed and implemented the New Business Acceleration Team, which consolidated and coordinated once-separate city inspections, so that new restaurants and retail stores could get their permits and open their doors more quickly. Before that effort, she developed the concept of targeted multiagency enforcement as the first director of the Mayor's Office of Special Enforcement, where she took on another seemingly intractable problem that required interagency cooperation: counterfeiting of name-brand articles of clothing in one of the country's leading locations of such sales, New York City's Canal Street. That initiative, the largest anticounterfeiting operation in the city's history, required consolidating the resources of four agencies in many operations, including raids on a single property with thirty-two separate stores, all selling fake luxury products, which the city dubbed the "counterfeit triangle."

In her job at the BIC, Hyman took over an eighty-one-person staff and agency dedicated to ensuring integrity among commercial waste haulers and market wholesalers—industries once known for deep penetration by organized crime. BIC licenses over two thousand companies. When she started as commissioner, determinations about the integrity of a particular applicant depended on data from twenty-seven unaligned and inconsistent databases, comprising more than five thousand data fields and one million pages of paper files.

Reflecting on her first weeks on the job, Hyman wrote: "It was readily apparent that the agency was sitting on twenty years of information and data with no discernible way of using it effectively. Systems barely talked, cases lived in hard-drive silos and performance reporting was cumbersome."[3]

Hyman set out to eliminate the paper, scanning half a million pages of documents, and deployed an enterprise data management (EDM) system—an approach, much more common in private enterprise, that integrates separate databases.

More important, Hyman began the process of changing the BIC's focus from processes (following steps to the issuance of a license) to its actual mission of ensuring integrity. The risks it had to fight no longer solely involved the traditional organized crime families. Instead, new criminal enterprises had evolved to take advantage of the inherent resale value of recyclable materials—paper, metal, and even grease waste. Honest providers of these materials faced increasing illegal competition from thieves, so Hyman decided to use the commission's massive quantities of data to guide a change in enforcement.

Hyman and her chief program officer, Joanna Weiss, examined forty categories of information, including data on companies that operate in the private sanitation and wholesale market businesses, data on people who operate in the private sanitation industry and wholesale marketplaces, and data on the fleet of vehicles used in these industries.

Thanks to EDM, the analysts could now see data from many different angles. Weiss says, "For example, with all data about a particular person consolidated into a single location, BIC can now see entire employment histories of industry members. In industries where a common tactic is for less-than-reputable individuals to shuffle between companies to hide their presence, this is an invaluable asset. Consolidating all data into a single system improves BIC's ability to identify bad actors, and ultimately to use scarce resources more strategically." Weiss and Hyman also coordinated data users, encouraging them to communicate. They formed a governance committee that included a representative from each practice area within the BIC and identified and met monthly with staff they labeled "power users"—those employees most active in using data to fight crime.

With assistance from the Mayor's Office of Analytics, using a "hotspot" analysis, Hyman saw that in addition to thwarting thefts, she could also help relieve a costly problem for the city's Department of Environmental Protection: restaurants were illegally dumping their cooking grease into the sewer system. Every restaurant is required to have a licensed hauler take its grease, so by collecting industry data on grease production, restaurant permits, and sewer backups from the Departments of Health (DOH) and Environmental Protection (DEP), Hyman's department could predict illegal activity and target enforcement. BIC, DOH, and DEP inspectors collaborated to identify which restaurants lacked a licensed carter, thereby identifying the restaurants that were either illegally dumping or participating in the grease black market. Focusing on the outliers produced dramatic results—an increase in enforcement actions of 30 percent while achieving a 60 percent reduction in manpower dedicated to grease enforcement.

The Renewed Public Employee

Stories like Payne's and Hyman's are encouraging illustrations of how much can be done when nineteenth-century governance is transformed with digital tools. But most of today's public employees still labor in the highly mechanized, routine processes of a government system created more than a hundred years ago. Consider, as an example, the case of the two thousand dollar ticket. As deputy mayor of New York City in 2010, Goldsmith encountered that ticket, which had been written by a Department of Sanitation inspector and given to a man who had picked up a piece of an air-conditioner from the street. The relevant law was aimed not at citizens who picked up a single discarded appliance but at organized gangs that stole valuable recyclable material that would otherwise have been sold by the city. However, no one in the system had any discretion. Any such violation, according to Sanitation Department regulations, mandated a violation and a fine of two thousand dollars. The system in which the inspector worked could neither provide him real-time information relevant to enforcement questions—Was the culprit a recycling recidivist? Was the junk valuable?—nor did it have the tools to monitor how he used his discretion. And thus he was not permitted to use his judgment.

It was just the sort of absurd situation that can and should vanish into history now that digital technology is widespread. With the ability to access information in real time, employees deepen their knowledge and can use it to inform their judgments. The instant flow of data also affords supervisors the chance to support, train, and monitor their field staff much more closely than they could have in predigital times. With that safeguard against abuse, workers can be unshackled from legacy rules that limit their discretion. In other words, pushing data to the field changes the nature of public work and engagement. And that, of course, represents an opportunity to revolutionize public work. A performance system based on learning allows for deviance: workers can make decisions about allowing exceptions, departing from risk-averse procedures when such departures would add value. It allows, for example, a Sanitation Department inspector to act on the obvious difference between a gang of thieves and an ordinary citizen picking up a discarded air conditioner. It is a new and better form of accountability. Like any other kind of accountability, it does not guarantee that errors will never be made, but it does increase the likelihood that workers will make informed, conscientious decisions.

As an example of how information flow can replace rigid routine, consider the San Diego Sheriff's Department, whose four thousand employees provide services to three million residents. For decades, when a deputy on patrol needed hard information, he or she would request it by radio from dispatchers and wait. Today thanks to a data fusion project, deputies can immediately get probation information, warrants, photos, and other important information related to a particular license plate or driver's license number. According to Ashish Kakkad, the department's chief information officer, the new data approach promotes the patrol officer to the role of "the decision maker rather than a mere conduit who transfers messages from the street to a dispatcher who secures information and eventually sends it back to the deputy." With rapid, well-integrated access to key data, officers make much more effective use of their time, Kakkad explains. The effects of digital tools ripple out into many aspects of the job. With information so readily available when needed, the department can now recognize the experience and knowledge of its employees, entrusting them with discretion to use their judgment. The new data tools can unlock dramatic productivity gains if the structures of government allow them.

The Digital Civic Switchboard

At a small office in Manhattan's Meatpacking District, the workers behind the nonprofit OpenPlans look for ways technology can help the public find bike-sharing locations, learn where a bus is on its route, and solve other daily urban dilemmas. They labor to produce online tools that gather public input and share information in order to make cities operate better. Although their methods are digital, the role the group plays in the community would be familiar to any resident of 1930s New York: they are the modern equivalent of the switchboard operators.

The switchboard operators of yesteryear did far more than connect phone lines. They managed the fabric of their communities. Births, election results, traffic accidents, and local gossip were their daily fare. They embodied the community's voice and its memory. In their ability to match a specific person's problem with the resource needed to solve it, they delivered solutions to individuals and encouraged their engagement with their neighbors.

After the demise of the switchboard, no one took the operator's place. Instead, the role of the civic hub was preempted by professional bureaucrats. Without a "switchboard," government officials made decisions (about which pothole gets fixed first, what restaurant can open, where a child can go to school) that were technically correct in that they adhered to procedure, but they ignored the community's collective knowledge. This process unintentionally marginalizes the people it was designed to serve, excluding them and their imagination from participation even in decisions involving their own families.

In the digital era, this bureaucratic system is bound to end. It will be replaced by people and digital tools. These hubs of community problem solving will use both city hall's data (made accessible to the public) and data generated by citizens themselves to tailor responses, engage and respond to problems, and even prevent problems from occurring in the first place. As the switchboard operator lived on the phone lines, these new problem solvers will live in social media—the connective tissue of community in our century. Of course, there will be differences between the new social media urban community and the switchboard of yore. Social media brings far more people together than the old phone system ever did, and unlike a corded telephone, these social media are ubiquitous and always available. Hence social media will break down barriers—between citizen and public servant and between citizen and citizen—and upend urban hierarchies.

Governments that embrace the digital civic switchboard will make it a platform for joint action with their constituents. Once this has occurred, cities will be able to better prioritize resources, anticipate problems, customize responses, and unleash the now-untapped resources of collaborative community action. Innovative governments will create new ways for citizens to make their voices heard, giving them the ability to provide input into regulations, budgets, and the provision of services. This new form of engagement will create better ways for residents to register requests for service or complaints. Beyond that, it will give citizens a chance to play a part in the design, and sometimes the delivery, of these services. An example: a few years ago, New York City created its Community Data Portal (an online trove of truly interactive, usable data maps) and gave training in its use to leaders of its fifty community boards (committees made up of active community people, each representing a swatch of neighborhoods). Empowered with information, these activists created a steady stream of solutions to their local problems.

Those kinds of results are good for urban politics, as citizens find they can engage and find solutions to their problems. But the digital switchboard is also good for the bottom line, as the federal government's General Services Administration's (GSA), the federal agency that primarily provides services to other government agencies, has shown. In 2014 the GSA received Harvard University's prestigious Innovations in American Government Award for creating Challenge.gov, an online portal for running challenge and prize competitions. Since its creation, citizens who use the GSA's digital switchboard, which lets federal agencies pose challenges and offer rewards for their solution, have solved more than six hundred problems posted on the site. Rather than issuing a formal Request for Proposals from experts, for example, the Federal Trade Commission posted a "Robocall Challenge," asking for ways to block illegal robocalls. The public responded with nearly eight hundred creative submissions. The winning proposal, a software filter called Nomorobo, is now deployed and benefiting thousands of people.

Also on the site, the Air Force Research Laboratory set up a challenge to solve the long-standing problem of how to safely stop fleeing vehicles. For the twenty-five-thousand-dollar purse, a retired sixty-six-year-old mechanical engineer from Lima, Peru, submitted the winning solution.

Leadership

Ironically, the passage to a much more open and fluid kind of governance will require determined leadership from the top of old hierarchies in order to break down the calcified systems that cities have inherited from the late 1800s.

In New York City, Michael Bloomberg took office as mayor after long years of experience in the use of data, and he created a metrics-driven mayoralty. Agencies agreed to cooperate to set up his proposed data analytics center and other interagency data initiatives. Yet almost all of them soon asserted legal, technical, and operational obstacles to full participation. Budget experts also pushed back, worried about costs. Lawyers cited vast numbers of rules (most from the federal government) that prohibited sharing of data. Within each city agency, its chief information officer would explain how only he or she could manage the complex legacy databases of that unit. Despite his mandate, his commitment to data, and a raft of first-rate appointees, Bloomberg would not have succeeded in making New York City a leader in data-driven government had he not pushed hard from the top for change. The lesson here is a bit paradoxical: How can leaders at the top of a hierarchy create the conditions that will replace that hierarchy with a far more open and fluid system?

The chapters that follow all contain variations on the answer to that question. They describe how elected leaders in major cities asserted themselves to break down inertia and advance the digital revolution in government. As we recount their stories, we look beyond the beginning of this digital revolution to consider its ultimate end: a new age of responsiveness in city government, where public servants perform truly valuable work in conjunction with those they govern. Unleashing the power of data and analytics will bring about the crack-up of the age of bureaucracy, allowing government to move from a compliance model to a problem-solving one that truly values the intelligence and dedication of its employees and the imagination and civic spirit of its citizens. In a sense, then, the chapters that follow feature an awkward growing-up period in which legacy forms of governance from the past unevenly confront the digital technology that will shape the future.

Yet this awkward age should lead to a great renewal in governance. Giving citizens confidence that government represents them, even in the mundane delivery of day-to-day services, will help position the country to address the overarching questions of quality of life, sustainability, resilience, social justice, and the like as the world continues to urbanize. As public servants in cities have long known, people care first and foremost about the lives of their own communities. This is why some of the most effective and most inspiring steps toward the responsive government are taking place in our cities thanks to the leaders you will meet in this book.

CHAPTER ONE

The Return of Retail Governance

As he describes his more than thirty years of tech experience, Bill Oates's Boston-accented words come fast and frequently. He has a shock of white hair that makes him look much like a younger Tip O'Neill, but Bill Oates is all boyish enthusiasm. He began his career as a telecommunications specialist for Sheraton Hotels—he was the "phone guy"—while he went to law school at night. He took to the work, becoming the hospitality industry's expert on telecommunications while rising through the information technology (IT) ranks at ITT Sheraton. After Sheraton merged with Starwood and Westin in 1998, Oates served as Starwood Hotel & Resort Worldwide's chief information officer for years. In the world of IT, he could handle anything.

But all of his years had not prepared him for what he heard when he walked into the IT department in Boston City Hall in the summer of 2006 to become the city's first cabinet-level chief information officer (CIO): the sound of typewriters.

Boston had a reputation as a well-wired and digitally savvy city by the time Mayor Tom Menino offered Oates the CIO job. "My biggest fear was that all the good stuff would have been done," Oates jokes. When he walked in and heard the clacking of nineteenth-century writing machinery, he realized, as he puts it, that government's organizations "take a long time to evolve."

Oates (who has what Lindsay Crudele, community and social technology strategist for the City of Boston, describes as a "particular fearlessness") doesn't discourage easily. His leadership style is unruffled, he's always ready with a good line, and he comes across as both energetic and unflappable. "Why is it so important for government to change?" he asks. "Because it hasn't."

When he was at Sheraton and Starwood, the companies had to adapt to survive. Consultants from McKinsey would show up every couple of years, soon followed by reorganization. The stock price would go down. A global epidemic would menace the hotel industry. Online bookings made inroads on hotels' former business model. There was never a year, or even a month, when the organization could ignore the prospect of change.

Government, Oates notes, seldom faced that kind of pressure to innovate until recently, out of necessity. When a tough economy drove Boston's budget down even as demand for city services increased, Oates told Menino that information technology wasn't a "would like to have" item anymore. Going more effectively digital was a matter of survival. "If you want to deliver great services to the people in this city," he told the mayor, "we have to do this differently. And technology is a critical part of it."

Oates, who had years of experience as a part-time elected official in his nearby hometown of Watertown, has a strong civic bent. He's a fan of Jane Jacobs, who famously argued that cities have to be made by their residents, not by plans imposed from above. Oates believes that cities can provide for everybody only when they're created by everybody. Hence, he thinks, city government needs to connect better with the people it serves. That was to become his guiding principle as he figured out how his new office would function. "With the mayor's leadership, his focus on people, and my ideas around IT," he recalls, "we started thinking about one word: *engagement*. How could we use today's technology to better connect with his constituents?"

In fact, constituent engagement was to become the linchpin of Oates's—and Boston's—digital success story. Between 2006 and 2013, with Oates as CIO and the mayor's strong support, the city adopted new digital tools and allowed its government to be changed by those tools, with impressive success. The story of how it accomplished this transformation, full of useful and disruptive lessons for other cities, begins with the ambitions of a nuts-and-bolts, decidedly non-techie mayor.

In 2006, when Oates joined city government, Menino, an affable man with an open, friendly face and a strong Boston accent, had long been famous for his tireless efforts to connect with his constituents. He loved to shake hands with the people he was serving, and he was always out in Boston's neighborhoods, indefatigably attending event after event. People liked to say he had personally met almost half the people of Boston (population 636,000), and a poll published by the *Boston Globe* in March 2013 found that 49 percent of Bostonians surveyed said they had, in fact, met him.[1]

Ever since 1993, when he was first elected after a few months as acting mayor, Menino has been known as an "urban mechanic" for his attention to the gritty details of city management, like snow removal. Oates says, "He wanted to make sure that the streets were clean, and that they were plowed, and that the neighborhoods were nice places to live. It was really all about people." (Indeed, in early January 2014, when a monster snowstorm bore down on Boston, Menino, just days away from leaving office, called it "a New Year's gift, to receive one last snowstorm as mayor.")[2]

It was his endless search for ways to engage his constituents that prompted Menino to look at digital technology. In December 2005, when he'd been preparing his agenda for his fourth term, he was told that technological innovation could provide new points of contact between government and its people. He decided to give the idea a try and announced he would bring on a cabinet-level CIO. For the first time in Boston's history, a digital official would be on the same level as the police commissioner, the school superintendent, and the other department heads. When Oates agreed to take the job, he found that its role was both well positioned—the new CIO would be reporting directly to the mayor—and completely undefined.

"I asked the mayor, 'What do you think I should be doing, boss?' And he said, 'I don't know; that's why I hired you,'" Oates remembers. Technology had never been the mayor's thing. "He was convinced by other people he trusted that he needed one of these guys," Oates says. Despite his new, citywide CIO title, Oates's department in 2006 was in fact more "City Hall Management Information Systems." They were well respected for supporting finance and administration systems and being responsive to PC, network, and mainframe issues when required. But "no one was really attacking [the question of], 'What do we need to do with technology to drive all of city government forward?'" Oates recalls. It would be three years before Oates was able to rebrand his office as the Department of Innovation and Technology.

And yet as Menino left office in early 2014, after an unprecedented five terms, his team knew that the CIO and his office had contributed a great deal to a remarkably successful mayoralty. A few months earlier, a poll had found that 82 percent of Bostonians said they had a "generally favorable" opinion of the mayor (that put him one point ahead of even the city's beloved Red Sox). When he stepped down, the *New York Times*, under the headline "Two Decades of Change Have Boston Sparkling," called Menino "an incrementalist who, with prodding and cunning and by exercising total control, nonetheless took advantage of national trends like the back-to-city migration and helped propel Boston forward."[3] While many of the mayor's accomplishments had their roots in his earlier terms, there was no doubt that in his last decade in office, technology had made city hall more responsive. There had been, for example, dramatic improvements to the Mayor's 24-Hour Hotline; the introduction of a Citizens Connect mobile app for constituent reports to the city; and the establishment of an innovation center in the mayor's office (called the Mayor's Office of New Urban Mechanics).

"The mayor's technology efforts were part and parcel of his opening up the city, making it livable, and earning its people's trust," says Menino's last chief of staff, Mitchell Weiss. Mayor Menino had been described in the *Boston Globe* as "an uncommonly intimate figure in a time when urban politics and American cities have become anything but," and his technology team had absorbed this insistence on the personal.[4] For all of them, technology was a cure for the governmental mistake of keeping people at a distance. The mayor's high-touch ethos had been translated into a high-tech world.

It hadn't been easy. When Oates had started as a new CIO in city hall that June 2006, the city hadn't been actively investing in its technology infrastructure. "Out of a one-hundred-plus million-dollar capital budget, less than half a million dollars was directed toward technology initiatives," Oates says. In order to create technology initiatives that would have an impact, he'd need the city to spend some money.

Unfortunately, many earlier IT projects at city hall had a bad track record: they tended not to get finished and thus also tended to show no return on investment. Boston's chief financial officer was wary of investing in needed technologies and infrastructure like fiber networks for the city, information platforms, and enterprise systems. At his first budget meeting, Oates had his head handed to him in front of his whole team. Not only were his early requests denied, but the entire enterprise was made to look unserious. He remembers his department's administration-and-finance manager looking at him wonderingly afterward, saying, "Bill, I've been here a long time. I've never seen anything as bad as that."

Worse yet, resistance to his ideas wasn't only about money. Oates also learned that he was up against the pain and agony associated with government's procurement rules. "I went in and immediately started thinking about the things we needed to do and needed to buy, and talked to the budget office, and then they said, 'Okay, here's your three hundred thousand dollars for Project X.' I said, 'Let's get going.' They said, 'It'll be a year and a half, two years, because we have to go through the procurement process and it's a Chapter 30 procurement' [governed by state law] or whatever. It was really frightening."

Oates remembers saying, "Give us a chance, and we'll show you how this investment is going to have value for the city, in the quality of the services that we're delivering, in how efficient the departments can be, and how much better the data will be." He needed, he says, "to overcome the conservative nature the city had about doing some of these more forward-looking things," and loyally mentions that Boston's fiscal prudence has served the city well over time. But when it came to technology, the city administrators felt "being prudent" equated to "saying no." Oates was blunt with the mayor and the chief financial officer. "All the city was doing was deferring investments that would need to be made, because we can't ignore this," he recalls saying.

Even the mayor, for all his talk about innovation, was concerned that Oates's infrastructure proposals would scratch some techie itches without doing anything tangible for the City of

Boston. "The mayor would say, 'What's this doing for me out there?' once again bringing the focus to the people that lived and worked in his city," Oates recalls. Initially, Oates says, he just asked for time. "You need to trust me," Oates told the mayor. "You'll be happy with what we're going to be able to deliver."

Although the mayor wasn't completely sold on all of Oates's ideas, their relationship nonetheless proved key to overcoming inertia and resistance at city hall. Oates made a point of meeting often with the mayor "to have the conversation about the things we needed to change." The two got along well. Oates jokes that because he grew up outside Boston, he "wasn't one of the 60 percent of the people who had personally met" Mayor Menino before he started as CIO. He teased the mayor that his home in Watertown was closer to city hall than the mayor's Hyde Park residence. Oates was part of Menino's fourth-term effort to bring some new ideas and outside perspective to his leadership team. Despite the hurdles, he had faith in the mayor's commitment to move the city forward in interesting and innovative ways.

Demand for services like subsidized housing, job training, and public safety was increasing across the city. From Oates's perspective, the only way for Mayor Menino to be able to deliver more services, given the fiscal constraints that the city had, was to take a completely different view of technology, the importance of information platforms, and the need for departments to share information. Oates's direct connection to the mayor made it possible to make these points about technology over and over again.

Oddly enough, the vagueness of Oates's job description also helped. Mayor Menino didn't have a preconceived notion of what his new CIO should be doing, so Oates was able to define his own role and "kind of get [his] feet wet in the organization," he says. He decided to build credibility for himself at city hall by showing good-quality project management, getting projects done on time, on budget, and "delivering what we said we were going to deliver." The first step was to build trust by improving the quality of service for the servers and systems that Boston's eighteen thousand employees used, "because if we didn't do that, we would never have the credibility to do the more interesting, bigger, more proactive, and aggressive things that we wanted to do that we knew were important."

As he worked on the meat-and-potatoes aspects of his job, though, Oates saw a choice opportunity to demonstrate how digital technology could improve services in an area that had long been dear to Mayor Menino: the city's hotline for citizens.

Customer Relationship Management Goes Public

Before the development of 311 apps and centralized call centers, whenever a snowstorm hit Boston, government had a simple method for allocating plows and salt: staffers in the mayor's office answered phone calls from constituents requesting help. Those staffers would then call friends in other parts of the government and ask them to pitch in with the citizens' requests. There were no follow-ups, no calls to note the completion of a request, and separate departments were connected only to the extent they spoke to one another by way of phone, memo, or informal personal contacts.

During Menino's term, the mayor himself was a frequent caller to the Mayor's Hotline, a twenty-four-hour service that launched in 1968, dialing the number (617-635-4500) at all hours of the day and night to report streetlight outages and potholes. Menino felt it was vitally important that a live person answer his and everyone else's calls. He long refused to permit voice mail use in city hall, because he didn't want people to get an automatic response of any kind when they called; the personal touch mattered a great deal to him. "Not having voice mail is incredibly inefficient operationally," says former chief of staff, Weiss, "but it's about the most efficient cultural symbol that you will find."

Then, one day, the mayor had a new mattress delivered to his house and the store followed through by calling him to find out how he had slept. Soon afterward, he asked his staff why the city didn't do the same thing for constituent requests. That kind of tracking would require technical updating of the hotline, and that upgrade would have to embody the mayor's obsessive focus on constituent services and personal touch.

Oates saw how he could make that happen. And, crucially, operating the improved hotline wouldn't cost the city more than it was already spending on the service. (One of the mayor's top goals was "improving city services at the same or better cost," Oates notes.) Moreover, he realized, those improvements would also end up improving officials' communications with each other. In his early days in city hall, he had been surprised by the virtual and physical barriers to collaboration. The hotline itself, he'd discovered, consisted of four people sharing space with Department of Transportation employees working on Boston's fifteen-year-long highway and tunnel project, the "Big Dig." When the mayor announced a plan to move Boston City Hall to the South Boston waterfront, Oates recalls talking to the mayor about the opportunity that such a move would offer. "Whether we actually move or not, I just want you to turn the building upside down and shake everybody out of it." As he recalls, "I had never seen a building exacerbate the challenge of fragmentation and poor communication. You literally can't even find where the other departments are in a building like this. It was horrendous."

The solution for the hotline, Oates saw, would have to be a city hall equivalent of private enterprise's customer relationship management (CRM) system. So he took some early work from a mayoral steering committee and agreed to lead Boston's first CRM project. (Since no one at city hall understood what the term *customer relationship management* meant before he got there, he rebranded the term as "constituent relationship management.") Oates worked closely on the project with two others hired by city hall in 2006, Chris Osgood and Nigel Jacob, who would later become collectively known as the Mayor's Office of New Urban Mechanics.

Nigel Jacob, a gregarious Canadian who had worked on several start-ups, had won Boston's first Urban Mechanics fellowship—a program to put talented young people into government, where they could learn the ropes and generate new ideas. Chris Osgood, a low-ego, collaborative Bostonian with a family history of civic involvement, had come into the mayor's office as a Harvard Business School fellow that same year. Oates, Jacob, and Osgood began working together on the CRM upgrade as a group.

There were other public sector constituent-relations systems already deployed elsewhere, so the trio commissioned the Gartner

Group, the technology research and advisory firm, to review those and compare them with Boston's current offering. Gartner confirmed the problematic divisions Oates saw in city hall, discovering, for example, "thousands of listings for City of Boston services in local phone books." Some cities, Gartner found, had mastered the back end—the service delivery component that allowed them to adequately address issues as calls for service arrived but often in a less-than-systematic fashion. Other cities had the front end covered. They had methods to manage the notifications of issues but often without a systematic way to address the problems and repairs. So Oates and his colleagues concluded that Boston needed a CRM system whose front end and back end were both robust and tightly integrated. Oates presented the team's vision to the mayor and quickly received his approval in early 2007. Menino announced that city hall was working on a new, improved call center.

Integrating the new technology into the hotline was tricky and took longer than expected. Mayor Menino was still the most frequent caller of the Hotline—often at 6:00 a.m.—and was not happy when he wasn't able to reach a person. The mayor would call his CIO and ask, "Billy, what are you doing to my hotline?" Oates would reply, as he often did in those days, "Mayor, just give me a little time."

But time kept passing, and the press became impatient. In April 2008, a *Boston Globe* story quoted "senior city officials" as saying, "It could be nearly two more years and $2 million more before the administration has a citywide system to keep track of residents' complaints."[5] Fortunately, the article merely stiffened the mayor's resolve. After it was published, the Mayor's Office issued a press release ("Mayor Reaffirms Dedication to Constituent Services and Hotline") and appointed a special assistant to the mayor, Patrick Harrington, to work with Oates to bang heads and get the project done.

In October 2008, the new CRM system formally launched. Within months, city hall was touting the new system's response to citizen inquiries as well as the speed with which city employees were performing repairs on public works. The system not only made it easier to report a problem but also possible to track when it was completed. "The length of time it took city workers to deliver new recycling bins, for example, decreased from a month on average last fall to just one week earlier this month," said a *Boston Globe* story in May 2009.[6] "City workers now fix burned-out street lights within a week, down from an average of 17.5 days last year. And park maintenance requests, which took an average of 10 days to be fulfilled last fall, are now being addressed within six days." Citizens were still calling the Mayor's Hotline in numbers to report issues like potholes or streetlights, but now they could also chat live with hotline employees online or use the city hall website's self-service option.

Today, follow-up—notices of work completion and follow-up e-mails and phone calls—is standard in the CRM system. "Contrary to belief, it's not really so much that the first impression is the most important," says Justin Holmes, Boston's former director of constituent engagement and current interim chief information officer. "It's really the last that lingers the most in the mind of our customer or in our case, the constituent. So what we do now, not only do we close the loop with people by e-mail—you report a pothole to us, you get an e-mail when the case is closed by the public works employee. And that affords you the opportunity to reply to us and have any further discussion that might be necessary by that report. We also pick up the phone and give you a call back every once a while just to check and make sure you're satisfied." Boston's CRM is so finely grained, in fact, that a citizen who makes a particular complaint can track its progress through the system—"like tracking a package," as Thomas Tinlin, commissioner of transportation, puts it. The constituent can even get a photo of the finished product.

For the mayor, the idea of technology that let the city reach more people was very appealing. Oates explained, "The mayor gave us his complete support through this whole thing. And in this city, I always say to people, when they say, 'Wow, how have you guys got so much done here?' I say, 'Because it's who we are and it's the way we're organized.' And you know, the mayor, in my view, is as empowered a CEO as any private sector CEO I've ever reported to, and so the fact is, it was a leadership issue. He was saying, 'This is how we're going to do things.'"

Yet all this change really only brought Boston up to the point where it required even more technology and more change, setting the stage for a project that would always improve.

Connecting Citizens via App

The year after Oates arrived at city hall, Apple had launched the first iPhone. A few months later, in early 2008, the company issued a software development kit for people who wanted to write apps for the device. That gave Chris Osgood and Nigel Jacob an idea: What if the city offered an app that allowed people to report graffiti, potholes, or other problems just by taking pictures with their iPhones? That was the seed of Citizens Connect, the first "mobile 311" app.

It was Osgood's and Jacob's ability to partner with organizations outside the walls of city hall that turned their idea into a powerful digital tool. In 2008, their first stop was the MIT Media Lab, where famed professor Hal Abelson knew of someone who had started a smartphone application development company—in those early days, such people were rare. The company was called Connected Bits, and Abelson introduced Osgood and Jacob to one of its founders, Dave Mitchell. Mitchell, who had worked with Microsoft Research and MIT, had gotten interested in mobile technology very early: he and a coworker, Eric Carlson, had launched Connected Bits in 2003. Even before the iPhone and its imitators, "we found we could do some interesting things on the phone and communicate it back to a browser," Mitchell says.

He recalls an initial meeting with Jacob, Osgood, Oates, and some city GIS staff: "So we [Connected Bits] were excited, did a bunch of work, and returned a few weeks later with a functioning prototype. We met with the same city hall people and showed a demo that captured a photo, added a GPS location and some basic information, and transmitted it all to a server for managing. And if you closed the request on the server, it would send a text message back to the reporting phone."

The city hall staffers were stunned, Mitchell says. "They're not used to that kind of turnaround, going from concept to visible functional prototypes between two meetings." But Connected Bits was nimble because it was a private company. That also meant it needed to be paid to develop the prototype. Unfortunately, Osgood and Jacob were offering just five thousand dollars, hardly enough for a functioning big-city product.

Luckily for Osgood, Jacob, and Oates, Connected Bits was generous. "We said, 'Look, this is what we've been working on for a while. And having a good partner and a use case and a reference is good,'" Mitchell recalls. "'So we'll do it for free.' But we asked the city to kick in twenty-five thousand dollars for support for the first year, because we knew that once we launched it, support is a continuing, ongoing thing." Oates agreed to that request on the spot.

When the app was deployed in the fall of 2009, it was cutting-edge technology. "Nobody was doing this," Mitchell says. The largest portion of the work was getting the application to work smoothly with the basic CRM system that Boston had purchased; integration took about six months.

Even as the team worked diligently on the technical issues that had to be overcome, they found that the problems they had anticipated didn't materialize. They had worried about protecting privacy and preventing abuses in such an open system, but neither issue proved important. As Mitchell recalls, "after a whole year and ten thousand reports going through, there were one or two slightly inappropriate things. But it turns out all of that worry was almost for nothing."

Citizens Connect provided an additional channel for citizen reporting that was both novel and, for many people, easier to use than a website. As Public Works chief of staff Matt Mayrl explains, Citizens Connect "slimmed it down, what previously was starting up a computer, waiting for it to start, loading the Internet, going to it, remembering the website page. It made that whole process easier. There's a little button ... there are four choices and you just do it." Justin Holmes believes that adoption and use of Citizens Connect signals that the city is now "tapping into a population that would not have been engaged ... previously had we not developed these new channels."

Chris Osgood believes Citizens Connect has "been a great service improvement and culture change for the city as a whole." Dave Mitchell agrees. He thinks the same culture change is evident from the constituent side as well: "What's really interesting is that people have said when they call in, they feel like they're complaining. When they use mobile, they feel like they're helping."

Citizens Connect also allowed the reporting of more useful and actionable information about each complaint or request. For example, a geocoded picture allows a viewer to zero in on an exact location and determine exactly the source of a citizen's problem.

That is a great deal more precise than a phone call about a "light out," says Mayrl:

> There was always that margin of error. Okay, is that a streetlight? Is that a light in a ball field? Is that a traffic signal that you referred to as a light? ... Now if somebody [using Citizens Connect] takes a picture of that, and it goes to the person whose job it is to know what the difference between all those different things is, and who might be responsible for this light, we get a much better higher-quality service.

The first version of Citizens Connect was focused solely on taking residents' reports. By the time the second version launched, in October 2010, the app allowed people to see on a map what other issues besides their own had been submitted and resolved by the city. What had begun as an app for service requests and problem reports now has the additional function of providing transparency. (Citizens Connect was in its third version as of fall 2013. Each version was subject to extensive testing by beta users.)

Michael Norton, a professor at the Harvard Business School, has found that governments that explain what they have done gain the trust and satisfaction of their constituents. It's a principle visible in many relationships that require trust: a pupil reassures a teacher when he shows not just an answer but the work that he did to get that answer. And Domino's Pizza adds to customer happiness by letting people on its website see exactly how their pie is coming along (down to the moment when the pepperoni gets added). In the same way, "showing your work" to citizens adds to their satisfaction with their government. Dave Mitchell agrees: "Usually cities are fixing as many things that come in and more, but most people aren't aware of that. And so [adding transparency] was a good PR move for the city, because people who used the system would see, 'Oh, look, I see fifty things were opened today, but I also see sixty things were closed today.'"

Connecting City Workers

In early 2011, Connected Bits released a version of the Citizens Connect idea for Boston's public employees at work in the field: an app called City Worker. Like Citizens Connect, the newer app ties constituent requests to points on a map of Boston and displays them on the screen of a mobile phone. City Worker also allows workers to respond to dynamically updated requests and even to close them on the spot. City Worker has been instrumental in changing the culture within the Department of Public Works. Four years ago, many of the department's workers had said having to use a computer at work would make them quit. Today they feel they could not do the job without the technology. It not only makes their workday more efficient, it also increases the scope of discretion they have in doing their jobs.

This is an enormous improvement in what had been a paper-based work flow system. In the past, suggestions for needed fixes would come into a traditional office, be printed out, and then be handed to a worker before he or she went out into the field. Mitchell describes this static prior system:

> And so city workers would arrive in the morning, get this printout, and then leave to visit the sites. Meanwhile new requests are coming in while they are out in the field. A city dispatcher might call them on the radio if it's important. But usually they would go out and fix things, and at the end of the day return with a piece of paper filled with little Xes and checkmarks and notes scribbled on it. And so somebody in the city would have to enter that into the CRM. So then the next morning, it all begins again with a new round.

With City Worker, by contrast, about two hundred Boston Public Works employees, many parks employees, waste management employees, and others have with them in the field a personalized perspective on their work, via Boston's CRM system. Mitchell explains it:

> Potholes, graffiti, or any of the common requests that come in via the system are automatically placed in a queue for the fieldworkers to work on. And they now have a mobile device [so] boom, it's going to show up. Here's your list of things to do ... And they can view the photos and all the details. They can reassign it. They can put notes in. They can take photos. They can finish the case and close it, all in real time. And so when new things come in, they can say, "Oh, okay, I'm doing this one and there's one right next to me." They can create new cases as well.

Commissioner of Public Works Joanne Massaro, who struggled at first to persuade her staff to use the CRM system, said that there was no such resistance when City Worker was added to the mix. "The more we could make it user-friendly, the more easily they adopted it," she said of her staff.

City Worker is quite user-friendly, as it avails itself of the same design features that work so well on apps that workers use in their personal lives: clarity, simplicity, and ease of use. Mitchell explains, "City Worker is very single purpose, one thing you can do. Here's a list of issues. Tap it, it says, do you want to inspect it? Do you want to close it? Do you want to assign it to somebody else? And if you say assign to somebody else, it says, well, who? Or where do you want it to go? If you say, new pothole, it will then ask you [for] just the pertinent information."

Workers who might have said "I'll quit if you make me use a computer" are fine with using that familiar tool of daily life, the smartphone. That comfort level made it easy for the Department of Public Works to make City Worker an integral part of the job and its performance management. And that, according to Mayrl, has yielded useful new metrics: "When we did the [CRM integration] and all this stuff could be digitized, we started measuring each of the district yards on the number of mobile cases that their inspectors created. And then we put in a system to track the number of hours that people were assigned to ... so we could manage the number of cases ... But the foundation was, we had one core set of data that was undeniably accurate and ... people were fully bought into [it]."

Public works fieldworkers began using City Worker in February 2012. Because of the app, says Mayrl, among other performance measures, pothole repair rates improved dramatically: in February 2011, only 48 percent of repairs had conformed to the department's service-level agreement with the public—two days from start to completion. In January 2013, that rate was 96 percent.

In the next version of City Worker, Dave Mitchell would like to add a view of real-time statistics tailored to the individual employee, displaying performance metrics for the worker, his or her district yard, and the city at large: "Because right now, two days before the end of the month when their meeting is, they all of a sudden put on a big burst of energy and go fix those potholes that are overdue.

And they all come in, bated breath, waiting to see. 'Oh, just missed it.' Or, 'Oh, yes, I'm on top.' But they really don't know where they are throughout the week. And so giving them a real-time perspective graphically of how they are in terms of their goals—individually and as a group—we think will be empowering."

Meanwhile, the planned next version of Citizens Connect will focus on collaboration between public servants and their constituents. Mitchell describes Version Four as a mini-CRM system: it includes a call center, allows city worker completion of tasks to be made visible, and generates reports. A dashboard will allow citizens to watch reporting at a neighborhood level and send triggered alerts to constituents. In other words, Version Four represents what Mitchell calls "grand unification"—making it possible for a worker to communicate directly with a constituent about repair options. Constituents may even be able to thank workers directly via the app. This version will be available to other cities, which will be able to license it and deploy the software for their own needs.

Bill Oates and Boston have come a long way since Oates started his job to the sound of clacking typewriters. The iPhone version of the Citizens Connect app has been downloaded tens of thousands of times and has been used to create tens of thousands of citizen requests. The Department of Public Works is operating more efficiently thanks to City Worker. And the creation of City Worker and Citizens Connect has arguably helped to generate reliable data for the Department of Public Works, which has led to much improved performance management by the department. Public Works is a more accountable place than it was before the advent of Citizens Connect.

This virtuous cycle not only makes government more responsive; it encourages city workers to use their initiative to solve problems and in return generates citizen trust and confidence—the civic glue necessary for all cities to prosper. As Alex "Sandy" Pentland, the futurist-thinking head of the MIT Media Lab, comments, "There is growing evidence that the power of engagement—direct, strong, positive interactions between people—is vital to promoting trustworthy, cooperative behavior."[7]

All of these lessons were not lost on Mayor Menino. It was the launch of the city's more interesting and innovative tech-based services—and Citizens Connect in particular—that made the mayor "very trusting" of the CIO function and the Office of New

Urban Mechanics, Oates says. And, in turn, colleagues credit the core team of Weiss, Osgood, Jacob, and Oates for finding a way to translate the mayor's focus on constituent services into digital tools.

The Next Step

Oates, of course, has a vision of what could happen next, including both a more truly personalized CRM system and a large step into the world of big data and predictive analytics. First, a city's CRM system could accommodate the urban government equivalent of a loyalty program to encourage citizen engagement in problem solving. "That connection with our customer is a huge deal for us," Oates says excitedly. "We're trying some things later that could actually credential, badge, and recognize people for reporting potholes, or for public workers who have done a good job."

Someday a future version of Citizens Connect may let a constituent know the name of the worker who fixed the broken streetlight on his corner. And the app may be providing the visualized data that citizens need to work with city officials to codesign plans for their community instead of just responding to pronouncements from experts and bureaucrats. Citizens Connect was the beginning of the beginning—a tool to further crucial citizen engagement. And that, more than its technical finesse, may be its most valuable contribution.

Weiss, for one, respects the way CRM has increased efficiency and generated useful data, but for him, the technology's greatest contribution has been to make it easier for citizens to participate in governance. "The biggest problem cities face are not efficiency problems," says Weiss. "They're participatory problems. They're democracy problems."

From the mayor's perspective, the CRM system represented a technological enhancement of his central philosophy. Even as the CRM system expanded to websites and smartphones, the sign on the wall still read "The Mayor's Hotline." Commissioner of Transportation Thomas Tinlin, himself a twenty-five-year city hall veteran who says he has always worried about technology replacing the "personal touch," said, "I see Tom Menino's fingerprints on the city everywhere I go, but I also know why he and, by extension, we, have been so successful ... We never relied on the old ways of doing business." The enhanced CRM system and the launch of Citizens Connect aligned with the mayor's strategic vision.

And the mayor's leadership was essential to getting it done. As the mayor puts it: "I never expected to be the mayor for twenty years. My first one, I had two newspaper stories saying that I won't last four years. I'm not handsome. I don't speak well. I didn't go to the right colleges and all that stuff. But I lasted twenty years. Not bad. I'm getting the job done, that's why."

When it came to his future, the mayor said straightforwardly, "My next life, I don't know what I'm going to do, but I'll make sure in my next life it's going to be all about people, how to help people. That's what we did here. And we did a lot of stuff."

As Mayor Menino's fifth term drew to its close, Bill Oates, Boston's CIO, was getting ready to move to a job as the CIO of the Commonwealth of Massachusetts. Although a key CIO role has traditionally been to provide technology infrastructure for the city, Oates believes that future CIOs will be stewards rather than providers: managing cloud services for servers and storage; harnessing mobile services in order to redefine how government can work for its constituents; encouraging employees to use third-party apps rather than proprietary services; ensuring that all of these third-party services are adequately secure; and, perhaps most important, "becoming incredibly proficient in everything around data."

Second, he says, digital technology could provide workers in finance and administration a window on police, fire, and emergency medical data. That would give the finance and administration people much better-informed views about resource allocation, he says. It's a natural extension to Oates, who, with his private sector background, often thinks of the city as an enterprise. The ability to make predictions—about crime and fire risks, for example—based on the very latest data from public safety data would lead to better decisions for the city as a whole. "We want this [data] to roll up so that we can make better enterprise decisions," he says.

As the digital governance revolution takes hold, Oates says, more and more cities will require their CIOs to be "great stewards of the data, both [data from] inside the city and other sources of data that allow our business users [city departments] to make smart decisions." Part of this transition, he thinks, will involve CIOs helping city departments to start looking at cross-agency data in a way that prompts them to say, "Boy, if I could get a little more of this data, I could be more effective." Right now, cities are "just scratching the surface," Oates says: "Everyone talks about big data. My view is that we're not big data. We're a lot of different data, but our ability to take that data, bring it together in interesting ways, and present it effectively to the folks that want to make decisions [will be critical]. [Data] will grow and become big data." Wise enterprises, Oates believes, find ways to manage others rather than build and maintain very complex systems.

He tells a cautionary tale from his early days on the job. His department had launched a project to make business licensing and permitting available in the City of Boston by way of streamlined online processes. The project wasn't a success, Oates says, because his team listened all too carefully to the city agencies involved, which wanted the digital system to automate what they were already doing. The resulting system ended up being an implementation of archaic processes. "As the system came up, it [became] clear to the users—because now they're seeing it in a computer system—they're seeing, 'Wow, this is kind of crazy how we do this stuff,'" Oates says. "So, [now] it's time to rip it all out and start all over again."

Oates now thinks this was a learning experience for him and for his organization. What the city had done with Citizens Connect needed to be done on the business-facing front for licensing and permitting: work with outside partners, find multiple channels for engagement (including mobile apps), do extensive user-based testing, and release new versions with agility. "All our organizations need to be more nimble," Oates says. "We need to do more of that visible testing."

There is, no doubt, still a long way to go. City systems still fall far short of what leaders can imagine. "We have to find better ways to solve the complexity of government," Oates says.

> The ideas around smart and connected cities are great, but implementing those solutions requires an enterprise view that is hard to find. We suffer from convoluted procurement processes that require us to prescribe solutions in detail and often limit our choice of partners. We also miss opportunities to effectively

collaborate across jurisdictional boundaries. The only way we're really going to change government is if we take our anecdotes about collaboration and turn them into something much bigger, so that we truly are sharing our resources across government jurisdictions more effectively than we do today. Today, individual government departments still try to figure out ways to kind of glue it all together, while the requirements change, and the parts kind of get separated from each other. And then you very quickly try to pull them all back together again.

The challenges evidenced by the release of HealthCare.gov are faced on a smaller scale every day in American cities.

But the city CIOs of the near future will have great rewards to match the great demands of the job, Oates says. Today creative ideas in governance are coming from cities more than from state capitals or Washington, DC. "We're being creative because we have to be," Oates says.

That's why Oates cannot imagine a better place to be than in a leadership role in the public sector on technology and innovation. There are so many tools available now with which governments can engage constituents: visualizations of cross-agency data, cloud services, social media (which Oates says is "instrumental for us in our conversations that we have with our constituents every day"), the power of mobility, ubiquitous sensors, and, coming soon, robotics and flexible displays on every flat surface. Technology and innovation, says Oates, are "no longer in the basement" when it comes to local government: "It's no longer in the back of the house. It's right there. It's at the cabinet table. It's in the mayor's office. It's in the governor's office." As is Bill Oates.

| Networked Citizenship

There you are, in line at the Department of Motor Vehicles. It's achingly slow, and the clerk in front of you clearly doesn't like people. What can you do besides commiserate with your fellow sufferers? Muttering, head-shaking, and eye-rolling may make you all feel a little less disgruntled, but they won't change anything about the way this government service is being (or not being) delivered.

Digital tools could write a new ending to this old and familiar story. They could, for example, give you a way to complain, while still in line, to the equivalent of a 311 center. Even better, they could afford you and your linemates the chance to publicly rate the service you're receiving, right after (or even during) the experience. As consumers, we are quite used to giving, and learning from, this sort of feedback (restaurant patrons, for example, do it all the time via the Yelp app, and drivers do the same in real time while on the road via the Waze app). As citizens, though, we have not yet experienced much of it. Unless we happen to live in Washington, DC.

There, thanks to a program called Grade.DC.gov, citizens can instantly evaluate the quality of services they have received from more than a dozen city agencies and the 311 and 911 call centers. Launched in June 2012 as a city partnership with a technology company, newBrandAnalytics, Grade.DC.gov collects citizens' ratings and unstructured comments, which can be transmitted through either a website or text messages. The system also mines Facebook, Yelp, Twitter, and the blogosphere for comments on city services. Finally, an algorithm quantifies and combines the data to generate an overall grade. In short, the project is a break-through effort to focus government's attention where it should be: the quality of services as perceived by the citizens being served.

This kind of digital change in governance can fundamentally alter citizens' relationship to their government. In Boston, citizens who reported problems to the city's traditional 311 call center felt they were complaining, but those who reported the same types of issues from mobile devices felt they were helping their community. For many, the power to truly engage with their government is a breakthrough.

Of course, there is room for improvement in DC's effort. For one thing, respondents are relatively few, and their small numbers may be skewing the ratings. For instance, DC's Department of Transportation was awarded an A on the strength of only 242 reviews in a city of nearly six hundred thousand. Even at this early stage, though, the grades and comments on Grade.DC have spurred operational changes, according to Mayor Vincent Gray and the staffers working on the system. Some grumpy DMV staffers, for example, have been moved into jobs that don't require interaction with the public. The mayor is happy with what's happened. As he told the *Washington Post* in July 2013, "It feels good to be a part of something that is different and new and I think has a refreshing amount of candor."[1]

In Boston, the Citizens Connect app expanded an existing channel of communication, the Mayor's Hotline, between citizens and city hall. Grade.DC.gov goes further: it creates a new form of responsiveness by government to its residents. But both of these channels were initiated by government. And if digital tools are to achieve their potential to create dialogue between citizens and government, citizens will have to not only use those tools but also develop their own tools that allow them to talk to one another about community issues without government's direction or prodding. Citizens need to develop a civic relationship among themselves in order to form a coherent community that is capable of having goals and a voice of its own—and of sometimes virtually marching on city hall on behalf of change.

Ever since cities first formed, a coherent voice of the people has emerged out of citizens' conversations with one another, not out of communications begun and defined by governments. And it's obvious that digital platforms can play a role in fostering those citizen-to-citizen relationships. As we shall see, the digital world is creating the tools to enhance such citizen-to-citizen communication in the streets of Chicago; the favelas of Rio de Janeiro; the brownstone blocks of Brooklyn; the suburbs of Austin, Texas; and the slums of Chennai, India.

Chicago

Daniel O'Neil wants to use digital tools to give a voice to people who aren't on traditional city government's map. "If you're not in the network, you're invisible," he says. "You don't matter. And everybody matters. Which means they have to be in the network. And not just on the Internet. But meaningfully. And not just meaningfully, but looking at meaningful things." Spiky-haired and fearless, O'Neil, who cannot resist cracking wise about any and all things, runs the Smart Chicago Collaborative (about which we'll hear more in chapter 4). It's a civic organization, founded jointly by the City of Chicago, the MacArthur Foundation, and the Chicago Community Trust, devoted to improving lives in Chicago through technology.

The collaborative's work revolves around three goals: increasing Internet access, improving technology skills, and expanding the innovative use of data to improve lives. Smart Chicago works toward these goals through administering programs and funds sponsored by its public and philanthropic parent organizations. One standout initiative is Connect Chicago, a program that has unified and expanded a network of more than 250 places that offer free computer use. Through administering the federal Broadband Technology Opportunities Program funds, Smart Chicago has upgraded computers and facilities and managed rollouts of computer training courses citywide. With more than 250 locations—and 195 of them that offer training—the program has made progress in bridging the digital divide. Another program, #CivicSummer, teaches teens how to use digital tools and become proficient in technology, media, and civic innovation. As executive director, O'Neil isn't shy about sharing Smart Chicago's mission and philosophy. "More than anything, we're about being open and inclusive, to everyone in Chicago and beyond," he says. "While we support organizations that help people through technology, we're not primarily funders. We're workers. We're practitioners. We're conveners."

Smart Chicago was the driving force behind one of Chicago's first digital-organizing successes. With its partners—a community group, the Southwest Organizing Project (SWOP), and a new start-up, LocalData—Smart Chicago devised a digital system that maps and reports dangerous conditions in buildings in Southwest Chicago in order to increase the city's attention to their need to be renovated. That creates new housing in the revitalizing neighborhood, replacing dilapidated buildings with homes suitable for families.

SWOP had been doing something similar, the old-fashioned way, since it was started in 1996 to "enable families to exercise common values, determine their own future, and connect with each other to improve life in their neighborhoods." SWOP members would walk around Southwest Chicago with pen and paper, making notes about vacant and abandoned buildings. Later, they would enter the data into an Excel spreadsheet, and then they'd use Microsoft Planner to put the information on maps to show it to other members. All in all, it was a pretty clunky system.

What brought the project into the digital age was the work of LocalData, a civic start-up supported by the Knight Foundation and Code for America. LocalData created a mobile app to allow community organizers to gather and organize neighborhood data and display them visually, using Chicago's already existing geodata. SWOP, O'Neil's team realized, could use this app to digitize their processes for tracking neglected properties. LocalData gave Smart Chicago a license to provide its software to SWOP—and made sure that SWOP would have technical support, unlimited hosted data, and the ability to allow an unlimited number of app users.

Gone was the era of paper notes and sitting later at a desk, navigating multiple pieces of software. Now, SWOP members simply use their phones to take pictures of problem buildings, automatically associate those pictures with their geocoded locations, and export the data in a form that can be forwarded to Chicago's 311 system. When they see a dangerous building where dumping has occurred or windows have been broken, they can flag the place, answer all the questions that 311 needs to route the service request, and know that this information is going in real time to the city.

This was not just an advance for SWOP. It was also a boon to the city government. After all, most city data on building problems arises from complaints and requests for service, notes Christopher Whitaker, the Code for America "brigade captain" in Chicago. A dilapidated building that's being ignored won't show up on that radar. This minor technological advance encourages the development of capacity in a variety of ways.

For one thing, it amplifies the voice of the community when it talks about vacant buildings; for residents, these lots are jagged holes in the fabric of the neighborhood, but these buildings aren't always the city's top priority. The technology serves as a tripwire, catching issues quickly and allowing for earlier, and therefore more effective, interventions. It simultaneously puts pressure on the city to react while adding resources to a city code inspection team that is always overworked: importantly, the method of reporting being used, which sends along pictures as well as complaints, assists the city in its decision making.

More timely reporting and an enhanced community voice also drive a more streamlined internal city process for handling complaints. The technology sets up a reinforcing feedback loop of communication as well: SWOP can check the status of its service requests for these buildings on its own website because the 311 system feedback has been linked to the organization's own operations. The result is a nimble and effective blend of organized citizens, start-up ingenuity, and local data. It's within the LocalData app that citizens meet and make their voices heard.

Community mapping has a long history as a methodology for engagement, and the potential of technology to generate dynamic, interactive maps greatly enhances it. A hallmark of Chicago's approach to becoming a responsive city has been the shared perspective that it takes a strong civic ecosystem—with public, corporate, nonprofit, and philanthropic sectors all pulling together—to ensure that new information and technology benefit all residents. Julia Stasch, vice president of US Programs at the MacArthur Foundation, recalled, "In Chicago, we realized that in order to fully tap the potential of information technology to accelerate every social sector objective we have—improving health and education, increasing civic participation, accelerating economic development, combating violence—we needed social sector leadership with a sustained focus on and expertise in the fast-evolving world of civic technology. That capacity didn't exist in any single foundation, so together with the Chicago Community Trust and the City of Chicago, we decided to build it. That was the genesis of the Smart Chicago Collaborative." Alaina Harkness, MacArthur Foundation program officer of community and economic development, added, "From its beginning, Smart Chicago has proven to be a vital force enhancing the information infrastructure. It's a catalyst, convener, and documentarian, bringing together, lifting up, and amplifying the good works of all of the different players across sectors and communities. Above all, it makes philanthropic investments smarter, driven by the insights and expertise of the Smart Chicago Collaborative and the experience gained from engagement with the communities we serve."

Rio de Janeiro

Favelas—the shantytowns that hug the sides of the steep hills above Rio de Janeiro—house 1.3 million of the city's 6.3 million residents. In the favela of Vidigal, on the Dois Irmãos mountain overlooking the Leblon and Ipanema beaches, two young Harvard graduates are determined to design and build spaces that will encourage civic participation—in the form of physical and digital activism—among the residents. Pedro Henrique de Cristo, who has an open, easy smile, was the first student to attend Harvard University from Paraiba, Brazil's third-poorest state. De Cristo and his wife, Caroline Shannon de Cristo, a top graduate from Harvard's Graduate School of Design with clear, piercing eyes and dirty blond hair, have moved into a two-room structure in Vidigal.

They are working on their plans to build what they call a "digital agora": a public space where citizens both make things and work on data about their communities. Eventually, the pair hope, each favela and neighborhood will have its own "physical digital space," where neighbors can meet each other, use a 3D printer and a laser cutter, and even write software. "Our goal is to make local interventions with impact," de Cristo says. "We want to take what was successful here to other areas of the city." Some of these agoras will be temporary pavilions; others will be permanent buildings, divided into rooms for different functions. All, the pair hope, will be conveniently located in the heart of their communities and served by gigabit Internet access. This is their aspiration. They have a long way to go.

Getting information on the Internet is increasingly essential, in favelas as much as in any other community, Shannon notes. Yet many favela residents struggle to get Web access. "The key problem is the connectivity," de Cristo says. "How can we improve infrastructure and services to connect these people, to make it easier for them to go to their jobs and have Internet access?" Just having that access will improve people's lives substantially, the pair says. But getting it through a space that promotes civic engagement will encourage those people to work together as a community. In the digital agoras, residents will be able to "articulate their ideas, propose what they want to do, and really raise their political bond [to each other] and political voice," de Cristo says. And, of course, when people are moved by this experience to become activists, the digital tools they need will be at hand.

One problem that such digital activism could address, the pair says, is the fact that favelas don't appear on any maps of Rio. Digital agoras could well become the means by which residents plan projects that use short message services, global positioning systems, and mobile apps that literally put their communities on the map. Digital agoras could also serve as the means for residents to interact more forcefully and wisely when the city government comes calling. For example, Rio's government is planning a cable car line to Vidigal and neighboring Rocinha and a sewage system for the favelas. De Cristo and Shannon want residents to use the digital agora as a convenient and welcoming hub for information about these projects and as a means for mobilizing informed residents to pressure the government to deliver well on its promises.

In fact, Shannon and de Cristo chose Vidigal for their first digital agora (and as their own home) precisely because the community has the strongest tradition of civic activism in Rio. They are being paid by private sector sponsors to design their concepts and construct their structures. Once their ideas are proven in partnership with the local community and the private sector, they plan to have city hall take over the units. They're optimistic about their timing: Rio, with the 2014 World Cup and the Olympics two years later, is being flooded with resources. The city knows it is going to be on the world stage for the next several years (e.g., in 2013, its mayor, Eduardo Paes, succeeded Michael Bloomberg as the chairman of the C40 Cities Climate Leadership Group). With the spotlight on his city, Paes, say Shannon and de Cristo, is interested in the world knowing that Rio is assisting its favela dwellers, and helping them to find their community voices is high on the list. Although they're determined to remain independent, they understand it is necessary to have the mayor's support and his authorization to use space in Vidigal for their first digital agora.

There's no question that Vidigal will be a challenge. For all its tradition of activism and spectacular views, Vidigal also has a long history of violence and drug traffic. It is not the easiest community in which to locate digital tools and promote civic engagement. But the challenges are an important aspect of Shannon and de Cristo's project. By 2050, fully a third of the world's population will live in slums. If digital tools are to become an effective part of city governance worldwide, then they must be useful to all city dwellers, including the poor and excluded. (Shannon and de Cristo's bottom-up work presents an interesting contrast to the city's top-down Operations Center, in which screens display information from 560 cameras, a weather forecasting system, and multiple layers of data gathered from sensors placed around the city.) While they work to get the digital agora done, they are applying its concepts to the existing Sitiê ecological park, a former sixteen-ton trash dump, which they along with the community have transformed into the city's first agro-forest and a global reference for public space, urban integration, and sustainability. That is the pair's ultimate goal: to furnish a way for these citizens to claim their seat at the decision-making table. Time will tell.

New York City

For a crowded place full of skyscrapers, New York City still has a fair amount of underused or vacant land, and a surprising amount of it is owned by city agencies. In 2011, for instance, the city's Department of Planning reported that the city controlled

596 vacant lots in Brooklyn alone. Paula Z. Segal, a lawyer, had recently learned that a vacant lot in her neighborhood was one of them. The parcel had been taken over by the city as a part of a vast public works project—the construction of a tunnel to bring water from reservoirs far north of the city—that began in 1970. Over the decades, she learned, the city had promised to let the community use the vacant lot, but nothing had come of those commitments. City agencies are often trapped by their own regulations and requirements (and limited resources) and put management of vacant land on the "too hard" pile.

Determined to change this status quo, Segal got together with Eric Brelsford, a programmer, to form a community group dedicated to liberating unused, city-owned lots. In honor of Brooklyn's supply of such land, they named it 596 Acres.

596 Acres took a good look at the public data on the Brooklyn parcels and found that the information was flawed. For example, as Segal told reporter Adrien Schless-Meier of *Civil Eats* in 2013, many long-standing community gardens were catalogued as vacant lots.[2] And some of those so-called lots turned out to be simply surveyors' errors. The group cleaned up the data, removing the community gardens and adding truly vacant lots that hadn't been listed. Then they checked the information against satellite imagery and Google Street View to be sure each lot was what it was reported to be. The group continues to update the data. Sometimes citizens write in to correct the map or report a change (people can sign up to "watch" a particular lot for the site). Sometimes 596 Acres learns new information about the history of a particular lot.

As a result, the 596 Acres website (596acres.org) is now a useful Zillow for abandoned land in New York City, with maps showing the locations of public vacant lots in Brooklyn, Manhattan, Queens, and the Bronx. The map is integrated with Google Street View, so by searching for vacant lots near a particular address, a user can see what things look like nearby. A filtering function allows users to look at all public vacant lots near an address, or public vacant lots that are already the subject of organization efforts. Clicking on a particular public vacant lot brings up details about the lot—its address, the city agency that has responsibility for it, and what (if any) community groups are using the land. Clicking again leads to the lot's own page, where users can set an alert so they receive an e-mail whenever information about that lot is added. Users also can add notes about what they've done about contacting the city for access to the lot or other steps.

Like many other successful digital-activist projects, the 596 Acres website provides information—much more accurate, contextualized, and relevant data about public vacant lots than activists could get on their own—and the means to get together with others who care about that information. The site's activism isn't confined to the Web. 596 Acres also spreads its information at the lots themselves by putting up signs. Under the heading "This Land Is Your Land," each sign gives information about the block and lot number of the parcel, tells how to reach the city agency responsible for the public vacant space, and provides the 596 Acres' own site. Neighbors who have been worrying about vacant land for decades now have a locus for action.

596 Acres has prompted more than a hundred efforts by communities to work with city agencies to license public land for a wide variety of community uses. Almost twenty of these campaigns have resulted in the land being converted to community-owned spaces. A loose federation of activists behind 596 Acres helps community organizers in a wide variety of ways, providing information about the process they'll need to follow to get access to land and walking them through the steps. And the city often (although not always) cooperates.

City agencies are often happy to license land through Green-Thumb, the city's community gardening program. In fact, the Department of Citywide Administrative Services is obliged to maintain its database of all city-owned and city-leased property with an eye toward finding out whether properties might be suitable for community use. 596 Acres will never lack for data, which the group will make contextual and actionable, building on the same model of accessibility that SWOP applies in Chicago. Citizens in other cities have enthusiastically adopted the 596 Acres idea, founding Grounded in Philly, Open Acres in Los Angeles, and Living Lots in New Orleans. 596 Acres, meanwhile, has begun working with private landowners to expand the data even more.

Austin

The creation of a community's civic voice is a local project by definition. But ideas, tools, and practical experience in one city can inform work in others. Kathryn Pettit, a senior research associate at the Metropolitan Housing and Communities Policy Center at the Urban Institute, is helping to make sure that successful strategies spread. A lively, cheerful, and bright-eyed woman, she is codirector of the National Neighborhood Indicators Partnership (NNIP). Her job is to coordinate organizations in more than three dozen cities around the United States that transform local data to create an invaluable long-term resource for their communities. The organization's mission is to help local people use the neighborhood-level information in policymaking and community building. Although Pettit is quick to say that the real work is done by NNIP's partners—"I'm just the conduit!" she insists—she's a crucial node in the network, ensuring that experience won in one place can help out in others. After all, one characteristic of digital community activism is that its projects often grow in unexpected new directions.

As an example, consider the story of Children's Optimal Health (COH), one of NNIP's local partners. COH began in 2006 as an informal cooperative effort among many organizations to share information about children's health in and around Austin, Texas, where the group is based. With leadership from the two largest hospital networks, city, county, and the Austin school district, the collaboration soon became an organization. COH helped the school district win a federal grant to work on behavioral health and antidrug issues, and safe-walking-to-school solutions in Austin. Their first role was to encourage agencies within the cooperative, including the school district, to share relevant data; COH served as the steward of the data, while organizations retained ownership. COH staff work to develop lasting trusting relationships with data partners, including legal staff and key administrators.

Achieving federal nonprofit status by 2009, COH's first project addressed childhood obesity, focusing on data at the neighborhood level. No one could deny that this was a major issue for the health of local kids: more than 40 percent of fourth-graders were overweight, and 23 percent were obese. Children's Optimal Health partnered with the Austin Independent School District, the University of Texas at Austin, the University of Texas at Houston School of Public Health, the Seton Family of Hospitals, and St. David's hospital network and pulled together nearly fifty other public, private, and nonprofit community partners in an all-out data-driven battle on obesity.

Texas state legislation requires that the body mass index and physical fitness of school children be measured by schools—in Pettit's view, an "amazingly progressive" set of requirements. COH, which had data-sharing agreements with over a dozen central Texas educational and health entities, focused first on helping its partners rigorously clean their data. Having made sure of its quality, the group then mapped the information, analyzed it—Where were those children going to school? Where did they live?—and layered other relevant data on top. Knowing where the children were located, the resulting visualizations could ask (and answer) questions like these: Where were parks, fast food outlets, green recreational spaces, grocery stores selling fresh produce, and transportation hubs? What were the socioeconomic and race/ethnicity facts about particular neighborhoods and streets, their crime rates, and available health services?

The dense, detailed maps that COH produced showed that obesity was a problem in all of the middle schools in Austin, but disproportionally concentrated in some areas. Because of COH's data-sharing agreement with the school district, it was able to show the neighborhoods where these students lived as well. Two neighborhoods outside downtown Austin had a particularly high concentration of overweight and obese students. (The maps also indicated that these neighborhoods had a higher proportion of fast food outlets.) COH published "heat maps" showing the number of overweight and obese children in particular neighborhoods, and the proportion of the school-age population they represented there, indicating disproportionate impacts.

The next step for COH was to organize community summits for their partners to come together to brainstorm solutions. COH's close relationship with the forward-thinking Austin school district helped make this step possible. Elected officials, faith-based organizations, health and social services providers, researchers, and school district representatives all met in November 2009 to discuss initiatives for healthier schools, more physical activities, and improved food supplies. At that summit, everyone talked about the causes of obesity, what interactions might be going on, and, as Pettit puts it, "really engaged with the data."

Of course, school-level interventions were an option, Pettit recalls. "Should you have more PE? What is the nutritional profile of the school lunches? What's in the vending machines?" But the involvement of so many different partners beyond the school system made more creative and innovative insights possible. "The smart part about the Children's Optimal Health obesity project is that it also realized that community-level interventions were needed," Pettit says. Mapping where the kids lived, their obesity rates by neighborhood, and the safe streets and fast food outlets around them made it possible to take many influences in their lives—from the stress of crime to the availability of fast food—into account.

Joint focus on a map that dramatically visualizes data is a great motivator that can help any group work effectively together on a shared problem. At the same time, more attention to the visualized data means less attention to rhetoric and emotion. As Daniel O'Neil of Smart Chicago puts it, his group is able to talk with people about difficult subjects like safe passage to school in "nonhot" (less emotional) ways by focusing on a screen. "And the ability for a focus on a shared interface to reduce heat is amazing." After all, one characteristic of maps that makes them effective communications tools is that they cross cultural, institutional, and language barriers.

Children's Optimal Health has found that insight to be true and is building on it. Following the community summit, the Michael and Susan Dell Foundation initiated investment in two of the high-need Austin neighborhoods. COH was able to leverage this philanthropic contribution and its focus on well-documented research connecting health outcomes to academic outcomes. That in turn helped the school district expand its middle school physical education program.

In recent years, improvements in student cardiovascular fitness have been noted, particularly in targeted hot spots. That has made other school systems, including those in suburbs, interested in seeing the sort of layered information that guided Austin. Obesity, after all, is not a problem confined to inner cities. Kathy Pettit, ever the careful researcher, is cautious: "These are really hard problems. It's not like, 'Oh, I see the data,' [and then] two years later obesity is not a problem anymore."

Instead of looking for magic bullets, she takes a longer view: to her, the COH project was one more advance in the steady building of a community's capacity to use data to govern itself. "To inspire people to do something, to identify that obesity is a problem. To start working on interventions and best practices, of which this project is a great example. And to track their progress." That capacity to use data, she says, is easily transferable. Now that the community is comfortable with using data to talk about children's welfare, she notes, it can adopt the same methods for other issues, like early childhood transitions to kindergarten or chronic absenteeism. "And that ability to use data as a tool in their mission and be comfortable with that is just really powerful, admirable, and, I would say, unfortunately not widespread yet."

Pettit often helps her NNIP partners, all local organizations from around the country, to meet face-to-face. Such networking "allows people to surface new issues and share ideas about mobilizing and about new directions for analysis," she says. Formalizing this peer network has been extraordinarily important in her view. "Being able to share new ideas about particular topic areas, like obesity, is the most immediate benefit. NNIP partner staff like Susan Millea and Mohan Rao from COH take their valuable time to relate stories, such as their work described here about obesity, because they know they will learn from other partners in other areas," she says. The next steps, she believes, are "really to push each other, to improve in our practice, to get more effective, to figure out better ways of organizing data, of sharing the data, and of mobilizing action." These local data-driven actors often do not have peers in their own communities, so sharing best practices and challenges and learning with each other make an enormous difference to their work.

Pettit finds such meetings inspiring. "People are doing amazing work and are really embedded in their communities, working to figure out how to help," she says. "They're making sure information is being used to improve conditions in low-income neighborhoods. This wouldn't happen without NNIP's explicit focus on democratizing data. It's easy to just write neighborhoods off."

Chennai

The slums of Chennai are some of those places that can be too easily written off. In fact, the Indian government has had little information on these slums or the people who lived there until recently. And even today, there is still disagreement over whether India's population of slum dwellers numbers forty-four million—or sixty-five million. One reason for the lack of clarity is that municipal governments divide slums in India into those that are recognized and those that are unrecognized. The government provides and maintains basic services in recognized slums and counts its residents as part of the national population. Unrecognized slums get few of those benefits. They get little government and produce little in the way of government services data.

Transparent Chennai, a nongovernmental organization founded in 2010, believes that this lack of data has allowed decision makers to duck their responsibilities. Like the other activists in this chapter, it is taking on this urban problem by producing good maps.

"Maps can be very empowering," Transparent Chennai's director Nithya Raman told *Forbes* magazine.[3] "They pose an incredible opportunity for people to write their own narrative about civic problems, their experiences of the city and their lived realities. They offer a means for the urban poor to represent their case against the official record, which may underreport or completely ignore problems faced by communities in the city of Chennai or any other Indian city." Ultimately Transparent Chennai aims to improve the lives of those living in the city's slums. The problems are fundamental: Chennai has only 714 public toilets for a population of 4.6 million, meaning that each seat is used by around 6,442—well over the established National Urban Sanitation Policy's limit of sixty persons per seat.

Transparent Chennai, which has been called a "collective of maptivists," started off with pens and paper, giving volunteers printouts from Google Maps with different sections of the city to mark up. The sheets were then loaded into a computer to create a master map that showed the services and basic amenities available to slum dwellers. Now the group has made the transition to digital, using open-source tools to collect data and create interactive maps about communal toilets, water supplies, garbage collection (or lack thereof), and sewage facilities. They're contesting and filling in gaps in government data in hopes of strengthening citizen demands for rights and entitlements. The group sends out reports in both English and Tamil aimed at catalyzing government responses and prodding community members to attend public meetings with local government officials.

Just as Children's Optimal Health discovered in Austin, Transparent Chennai has found that politicians react better to maps than data in charts or graphs. As Nithya Raman told *Forbes*, "Initially, the maps confirmed a story of neglect. But then they served as a basis to challenge that story. In the areas we mapped, we now see water taps and toilets repaired, providing better sanitation than ever before. Garbage is also collected and we even saw the clearance of a huge trash pile which hadn't been addressed in decades."

The Future of Civic Voice

Detroit and Baltimore have led the way within the United States when it comes to understanding and taking on urban blight using data. Detroit's Blight Task Force, sending over two hundred people across the city over the course of fourteen weeks, surveyed virtually all of the city's nearly four hundred thousand properties by collecting and wirelessly sharing detailed data about the conditions they found. Baltimore's mayor, Stephanie Rawlings-Blake, has launched Vacants to Value, a program that aims to create holistic solutions for entire city blocks based on detailed, layered, and aggregated data about the city's assets.

Communication among citizens about civic issues and between constituents and city hall will increase in volume and value. It started with texting or e-mailing a request for service into city hall and has evolved into the use of smartphone apps sending along geotagged images as well as text. But simply learning how to complain to city hall more effectively is clearly not the pinnacle of community involvement, and the use of digital technology to enhance communities' independent voices is still in its early days. What we have described in this chapter are some of the first experiments. SWOP, LocalData, and Smart Chicago have found a way to amplify and focus the input of community members to address specific physical problems in their city; Pedro Henrique de Cristo and Caroline Shannon de Cristo, in Rio, want to provide physical meeting places that will catalyze digital civic engagement; 596 Acres is making public data actionable by community groups and facilitating organization efforts; Transparent Chennai is using maps to drive attention to a population that had been invisible.

Showing people that they have something in common is the easy part. (Even people who happen to be waiting on the corner for the Walk signal have something in common.) But to have real leverage, a group must develop its collective voice so that it can't be ignored.

We think future civic groups will be using data and the graphical, networked screens fed by this data to create persistent civic voices that are worthy of widespread respect, and we'd like that moment to arrive sooner rather than later. When civic groups are more like coherent entities than people standing on a street corner waiting for the light to change, they can more effectively use data to work for changes in their cities that will make many lives better.

What turns a group into an entity worth respect? Part of the answer is memory—the ability to reflect collectively on the past and carry a sense of shared identity into the future. Another element is intentionality, or having an interest in carrying out a particular plan. Still another necessary element is the ability to assign roles that can be filled by different individuals: someone who can speak for the group, or manage it, or keep the books. If the roles stay more or less constant, the group can be coherent and ongoing, even though different people fill those roles. All of these elements—collective memory, execution of plans over time, the organizing of roles—should be implemented in civic software, which can make community voices clearer. And as we describe in chapter 3, a responsive city can listen better to clearer voices.

Civic software can also help address the psychology of groups, where scale matters a great deal. It is a fascinating and important fact that work gets done most efficiently in groups of about twelve people. At that size, a collection of people can have multiple channels of easy communication (think of a dinner party, with its flow of conversations whose participants change). In larger groups, people can fall into the one-talking-to-all broadcast model. That's fine for a lecture; it's not so effective for gleaning information from a community and getting its members to find solutions to their problems.

Social scientists tell us that each individual can know about 150 people as true friends. Most of us don't have the capacity to feel intimately acquainted with more people than that. The rule of 12 and the rule of 150 both point to the same lesson: community groups need to keep their work on a small scale. Yet they also need to combine with other groups to create larger-scale shared voices. Software could resolve that paradox: it could be designed to keep people focused on the local but give them an easy way to scale up and find partners in their or other communities.

Imagine civic software that would help smaller neighborhood groups get work done, assign roles, and keep track of their collective memories and their collective intentions for the future. Imagine too that this software would let groups combine themselves into larger entities (groups made of smaller groups) when they were ready. Such software would make possible a new kind of civic voice: genuine, independent, and digital. We think such software will be created. Its fuel will be civic data—from government and from citizens who have created the data themselves. From effective civic voice will come more responsive government. And the trust created as a by-product of this responsiveness will make civic voices more constructive and the results more lasting—for everyone.

CHAPTER THREE

The Interactive City

As anyone who has worked in a city hall can confirm, the place often feels far from Lincoln's beautifully simple definition of democratic government—"of the people, by the people, for the people." "For the people" doesn't fit the work of bureaucrats who don't listen to those they are supposed to serve. "By the people" doesn't describe policies crafted by experts without local knowledge or input. "Of the people" doesn't suit a government that engenders disengagement and apathy. This situation is not the fault of public servants, the vast majority of whom took their jobs with a desire to work for their community. Nor does the blame lie with elected officials, who seek and win office with the best of intentions (and find their idealism worn down by the obstacles they face). It is, rather, the underlying structure of twentieth-century government that often effectively sidelines the people government is supposed to serve (as we discuss in chapter 7).

Government's bedrock authority for action derives from elections, where the public expresses its will. But an election never provides sufficient direction to decide the thousands of policy questions that a city government must resolve in a typical year. Marching on city hall may generate some noise and cellphone video, but true engagement takes more time and commitment. It requires that people create and sustain a collective voice—a representation of a community that has true identity and thus the authority to speak "for the people." The century-old model of city government did much to discourage such voices. Now, twenty-first-century digital technology will foster them.

Accessible, well-visualized data is ending government's monopoly on information and authority. An important part of the digital revolution in governance will be the use of those tools by ordinary people to engage their government in ways that were unimaginable only a few years ago. We think that engagement will create a new kind of civic life in which government and its citizens will work as true partners to solve urban problems. That in turn will encourage people to see themselves as active citizens rather than passive consumers of services. Digital tools will help bolster existing communities and define new ones. And for both, information technology will help to create the sort of persistent civic voices that can make city government "of the people, by the people, for the people." These civic groups will have the characteristics we have described as essential for a civic voice: collective memory, the ability to plan and execute the plan over time, and the capacity to assign different working roles to members. In such groups, civic engagement leads to what policy experts label coproduction—residents and professionals working together as equals on civic issues.

Information technology can do more than aid existing communities in finding their civic voice. Even as they help recognized neighborhoods and associations, digital tools also create a new type of community—one whose members don't live near one another. Take, for example, the annual New York City BigApps competition. It's a New York Tech Meetup event, which promotes government transparency and innovative new technologies. Gathered in a shiny, modern Manhattan office building, hundreds of young entrepreneurs compete to see who can help the most New Yorkers solve a problem. In 2013, for example, the winner, ChildCareDesk, designed an Android app to help parents find quality child care centers using detailed information provided by various city accreditation agencies. Another contestant, Helping Hands, is an app that uses city data to assist New Yorkers applying for a variety of social benefits. "It's easy to lose hope when faced with the daunting task of finding and browsing through all the information related to applying for benefits," says Madelena Mak, who sounds like the city human services commissioner but is in fact one of the app's creators.[1]

Similarly, inventors Jeff Novich, Toby Matejovsky, Rory Pettingill, Andrew Pinzler, and Christopher Kennedy sound like the city job training office when they proudly show off their app. It makes it easy to discover, connect, and apply to thousands of jobs at two thousand New York-based start-ups and small companies. These entrepreneurs suggest how digitally engaged citizens come to see themselves as facilitators of public services, not just as consumers fighting for a bigger share of the municipal pie.

We are not suggesting that only the digitally expert will form such new communities. Quite the contrary—digital tools can help any citizen find others who share his or her concerns and motives to act. As an example, consider the National Archives and Records Administration's online Citizen Archivist Dashboard. Archives employees have an immense backlog of work, but thanks to the dashboard, a diffuse community of people is now helping to tag and transcribe materials and contribute to historical articles. The National Archives hopes it can work in partnership with these scattered but interested citizens to speed up work flows and get around budget constraints. In turn, citizens contribute to the work their government is doing in areas those individuals care about, with an ease that would have been impossible without digital coproduction.

It's important to understand that the new civic voices we envision will not be limited to an electronic update of the familiar urban pressure group, rallied by organizers to squeeze more services out of government. Such organizing techniques have long encouraged people to see themselves as consumers of government's offerings. Citizenship, however, involves more than the consumption of public goods. As Vincent Homburg, a professor of public administration at Erasmus University Rotterdam, observed, "A focus on service delivery (and a focus on the consumer rather than on the citizen) narrows the multidimensionality of citizenship and public administration and may therefore decrease legitimacy. The challenge for e-government is to develop participative forms of electronic service delivery and to address citizens at the same time as their identities as consumers."[2]

Whereas consumers demand more services from government, citizens demand more participation. Of course, digital advocacy to correct inequity in the allocation of the quantity or quality of public resources certainly will play an important role; we argue, however, that a focus on this goal limits the benefits flowing from engaged citizenship. Cities benefit when residents leave that first mentality behind and adopt the second. Digital tools, it turns out, are a good way to create that transformation. The reason is that those tools eliminate the data asymmetries that leave government holding all the cards while citizens struggle to engage with the issues that concern them.

In our years of public life, we have often heard civic leaders shouting in outrage because some study or report had convinced the policy elite to ignore their people's requests. As recently as a decade ago, planners made decisions based on information available only to them, then shared those decisions with the community. But in the years between Goldsmith's time as a mayor (of Indianapolis, from 1992 to 2000) and his time as a deputy mayor (of New York City, from 2010 to 2011), that top-down approach to city planning began to change. The cause was the open data movement—a push for the principle that data should be available to all who have a use for the information (especially if that data was generated by those who wish to use them).

When that idea began to percolate in government in the late 1990s, many feared it would merely engender a lot of facile "gotcha" journalism. Once the entire budget is online, after all, it's easy to cherry-pick the story of the Pentagon's inventory of five-hundred-dollar hammers. As time passed, however, government officials saw much more of the positive side of the movement.

Consider the story of Joe Morrisroe, the capable, hard-working executive director of New York City's 311 center. Morrisroe went along with city policy and provided datasets and software tips to community groups so they could access 311 data. But open data worried him. After all, his shop is the object of twenty million complaints and requests for information a year (a fair number of these are second calls complaining about the status of the first complaint). He doesn't get many compliments, and he expected open data to make his life worse. Using his information, people could call up a map on a computer screen and see, by the size of a yellow dot on the screen, how many complaints had been registered for any place they cared to look up. Worse, by merely hovering the mouse over the dot, neighborhood advocates could see exactly the nature of the request and how long it took to resolve it or whether it remained unresolved. It seemed perfectly designed for nitpickers and shouters.

But Morrisroe was pleasantly surprised by his first webinar for community groups on the new graphics display. For one thing, the groups were impressed and appreciative, and he finally received some compliments. More important, they were eager to use the data to solve problems. And they had plenty of proposed solutions that had escaped city agencies. As residents of a lively, complex neighborhood, the participants saw patterns that were not obvious to the city workers assigned to a single agency.

Wherever government data has been opened, the results are similar. The data has given citizens a better understanding of what government is doing—they can see the facts and reasoning behind those once-opaque decisions about stop signs, bike lanes, or zoning changes. The data also allows groups to participate actively in planning—citizens can approach planners with insights that the planners would not otherwise have had. When a city's data is easily understood, well visualized, and capable of being sorted and evaluated, data asymmetry becomes a thing of the past. That city's government will now learn as much from its citizens as its citizens learn from it.

Data asymmetry had let officials ignore community voices by not listening early enough or not helping those voices to be informed. As the economist Albert O. Hirschman argued in his classic book, *Exit, Voice, and Loyalty*, residents who are dissatisfied with their municipal government may respond in one of two ways.[3] They may assert their voice by complaining or proposing improvements. Or they may exit, withdrawing from the community and disengaging from civic life. In some cities, this exit was literal: citizens with the means would simply move away.

Every such disengagement, by a group or an individual, removes part of the fabric that knits urban residents into a cohesive community. And that fabric is essential to the success of a city. The Soul of the Community, a 2010 project of the Knight Foundation and Gallup, calls it "community attachment":

> Community attachment is an emotional connection to a place that transcends satisfaction, loyalty, and even passion. A community's most attached residents have strong pride in it, a positive outlook

on the community's future, and a sense that it is the perfect place for them. They are less likely to want to leave than residents without this emotional connection. They feel a bond to their community that is stronger than just being happy about where they live ... Across the 26 Knight communities, those whose residents were more attached saw more local GDP growth. This is a key metric in assessing community success because local GDP growth not only measures a community's economic success, but also its ability to grow and meet residents' needs.[4]

Good governance is not what creates this glue of civic attachment. Rather, it is civic attachment that creates good governance. This is why the digital revolution in governance will lead to a much better relationship between city hall and the people it serves.

Digitally Enhanced Democracy

The easiest way to grasp the benefits of an engaged citizenry might be to compare digital engagement with the kind of communications that have typified city government for the past few decades. Consider this tale of two meetings.

One morning during his tenure as deputy mayor of New York City, Goldsmith sat in city hall with Dennis Walcott, the newly appointed chancellor of the city's Department of Education. The two men watched news coverage of a marathon community event that Walcott had attended late into the night before. On the monitors, a series of upset speakers, one after another, told the unfailingly polite and self-effacing Walcott exactly how little they thought of his policies. There was plenty of angry talk, but little tangible progress on any of the difficult problems of finances and school performance facing the district. The event had no civic glue.

These large-scale meetings have long been a standard part of big-city politics. Occasionally they generate insights, but mostly they produce performances. Although the advocates are officially speaking *to* public officials, they are really talking *through* them. The speakers' real goal is to impress and move the audience to support their cause, not to work in any constructive way with the public servants who listen to them.

We will be the first to admit that this loud and theatrical ceremony is probably the result of a long tradition of meetings in which the professionals from city hall really did not listen, having already decided on their course. As urban problems became more complex and city workers became more professionalized, many community meetings evolved into this unproductive form: officials who did not listen, being yelled at by advocates who were not addressing them anyway.

Contrast Walcott's rough evening with a different experience Goldsmith had during his New York tenure. Goldsmith would convene three meetings a week in different boroughs. Each meeting was held in a particular neighborhood and focused on that community's concerns. Each was attended by fewer than twenty people—small business owners, parks advocates, community board leaders, and interested residents, usually crammed in a threadbare second-floor conference room barely big enough to contain them and their coffee cups. One of the first of these, in the Bronx, followed what turned out to be the typical course. First, the group seemed nonplussed that the city officials did not have a formal presentation, just a simple question: How could local government perform better? In their answers, the citizens' street-level knowledge complemented and enhanced that of even the best-trained technocrat. The first person to answer spoke about the location of the bus stops and trash bins. She had barely finished when the group, residents and officials, began to work out a solution to the problem.

A similarly refreshing sense of shared practical problem solving characterized an online program at New York City's water department (the Department of Environmental Protection). One of the agency's goals was to reduce sewer-overflow problems by creating green spaces, where soil would absorb rainwater and thus reduce storm runoff into the sewer system. City engineers did not sell a predetermined solution to the community. Instead, they specified the problem to be solved, identified the areas of the city especially in need of mitigation, and offered small prizes for neighborhood-generated solutions. Using both a specialized website, Change By Us ("a place to put your ideas into action by creating projects and building teams to make your city a better place to live"), and its own site, the department involved New Yorkers in deciding what kinds of green spaces would be built and where they would be located.

These experiences suggest how digital tools can make urban democracy more effective and bring it closer to Lincoln's ideal—"of the people, by the people, for the people." First, liberating data frees it from constraints of bureaucratic management. Instead of reports full of already-out-of-date information gathered by one department, community groups in New York now work with real-time data from many sources. That keeps the information relevant and the focus on problems rather than jurisdictions. Second, government's authority comes from its cooperation with a vibrant community, and the community's respect for that authority flows from government's responsiveness. It's a continuing loop of respect and efficiency. Third, and perhaps most important, in digital governance, communication is no longer one-way, from government's experts to the people who must live with their decisions. Rather, the new forms of engagement involve collaborative exchanges among technically proficient public employees and residents.

Such has been the experience of a few groundbreaking New York City Council members. In New York, council members are intimately involved in the allocation of social service spending in their districts. The discretion that council members exercise leaves plenty of room for favor trading, political revenge, and the occasional scandal. In 2012, though, City Council members Jumaane D. Williams, Brad Lander, Melissa Mark-Viverito, and Eric Ulrich decided to give their constituents a seat at the funding table. The four council members allocated six million dollars in discretionary capital funds by holding a series of meetings where community members proposed projects, debated their merits, and made their choices by voting. Over eight thousand people in these four districts participated, choosing to fund a variety of improvements from public school bathroom renovations to pedestrian walking-path repairs.

This approach, originally devised in Brazil and called participatory budgeting, is now in its third year in New York, with nine of the city council's fifty-one members using it in their districts. Between September 2013 and April 2014, residents decided how to spend twelve million dollars in capital funds. Chicago now has a similar program.

Participatory budgeting in both cities, however, remains a time-intensive commitment, involving a long series of face-to-face meetings and committee sessions, with votes counted on paper ballots. Neither city has yet made the leap to online deliberation and voting. In San Francisco, though, Mayor Ed Lee and city supervisor David Chiu want to bring digital tools to the process. The proposal is still in early stages, but this next innovation in participatory budgeting could clear a path for wide (and low-cost) adoption in cities across the country.

A digitally informed city does not limit its benefits to citizen-to-government relationship but also produces benefits in the consumer-to-business-world as government more completely considers information and knowledge as one of its most critical services. Accessible city government data can help consumers in many nongovernmental contexts. It can, for example, tell them which retailers have imbalanced scales, which restaurants have records of health excellence, where the bad traffic is right now, and so on. City hall can reduce the transaction costs of getting information and thus add to the productivity and quality of life of its citizens in ways outside the scope of traditional government.

An open government does in fact help its citizens consume more smartly. A good example of this benefit is Data.gov, which contains over four hundred datasets and resources from dozens of agencies across government. In addition to the raw datasets, the site features a number of apps that have already leveraged available data to help consumers make better choices—for example, College Navigator, Alternative Fuel Locator, and Find a Health Center. In the words of Data.gov, "Properly functioning consumer markets depend on consumers' ability to make informed choices."

Supporting Engagement

Of course, there is no urban problem so simple that it can be solved just by throwing technology in its general direction. Social engagement requires the right supporting infrastructure and design. To be specific, it requires five characteristics: well-visualized data, savvy intermediaries, a governmental platform that works, personalized responses from city hall, and resulting real-time information.

A Visualized and Usable Open Data Platform

Truly collaborative planning requires that data be contained in usable, well-visualized formats. Easily accessed and understandable open datasets give the broader public the means to work with well-prepared professionals who have better access to technical information. Therefore, it is not enough to simply open the data to the public. We were reminded of this recently when we met with budget officials of a city who showed us what they called their "open data" spreadsheets that would intimidate all but the most hardened CPA. Usable open data is packaged in a way that suits nonspecialists' needs. For example, the city of Palo Alto's online budget opens up with a dynamic six-color graph that provides both city employees and residents with the visualization tools they need to truly understand and analyze the numbers.

Digitally Savvy Intermediaries

Lack of technological skills can be a formidable entry barrier to participation in digital governance. Not everyone, after all, is at ease with dynamic graphs or even with websites and tweets. It is important, then, that digital governance efforts work with nonprofits that are both proficient in design and savvy in digital advocacy. These intermediaries come in many forms. One that concentrates on technology might help translate data into insights. Or a community development corporation might simply employ a person at ease with social media and digital mapping in order to better mobilize its community. A different community group could use different tech tools to identify new residents and work to attach them to community social offerings and support groups. At the same time (because everyone is a member of more than one group), that same new resident may also be part of an issue-oriented group (improve our schools!), and a different nonprofit might provide data on school quality or needs. Once the data has been opened up by a city, many different intermediary organizations can use and improve information concurrently to deepen participation and connections and foster joint problem solving.

Well-off neighborhoods are used to the experience that academics label coproduction, where citizens and government officials work together as equals on problems. Margreet Frieling, Siegwart Lindenberg, and Frans Stokman wrote in "Collaborative Communities through Coproduction": "Neighborhoods with high levels of livability are generally clean, safe, with well-maintained dwellings and other buildings and with residents being respectful of one another and each other's property."[5] Upper-middle-class neighborhoods might engage around such issues as traffic, national or regional issues, or recreational programming or be so secure about their neighborhood that they engage more frequently about other national policy issues. But residents in stressed neighborhoods often need more basic civic glue to be in place before such engagements become possible. Research shows that cooperation among residents plays a key role in achieving positive change in an urban neighborhood. Some neighborhoods, though, need assistance to get cooperation restarted after it has declined. Social media and the digital switchboard (described in the Introduction) can provide some of the attachment that these communities would otherwise lack. The necessary qualities of "self-help, mutuality, and trust often lacking in disadvantaged neighborhoods" can be buttressed through digital interactions.[6] Such help requires both effective intermediaries and government committed to designing the tools necessary for engagement.

A Platform for Engagement

In most cities today, when a resident calls city government to complain—say, about the weeds in a vacant lot nearby—a public employee at the contact center enters a request for service. When the person's neighbor calls on the same subject, the city call center makes another entry, totally unrelated to the first one. There is no mechanism to tell each neighbor about the other or to let either one know about the community group organizing a Saturday morning cleanup.

Boston's Citizens Connect, the iOS and Android app whose story we told in chapter 1, points the way toward the next evolutionary step for call centers. Citizens Connect is not just quicker and more informative than a complaint line. As we noted, the system also makes people feel better about participating. Those using the app report a higher sense of satisfaction in city hall responsiveness than do those calling 311 on their phones. That satisfaction helps foster a sense of ownership and loyalty, which is good for civic life overall (most 311 reporting happens within two hundred feet of the complainant's home).

The next step in 311's digital evolution is to socialize information, giving citizens the means to communicate and collaborate with each other on the issues they are reporting. Chicago and New York are now building new 311 centers that will permit this kind of contact among callers (who of course will be using multiple media, not just phone calls, to report their issues). The new systems will also "listen" to social media, and thus will not need to wait for a formal request for help to 311 before they act. And, of course, social 311 will be a rich source of open data that can inform residents about issues in their communities and provide them with the information they need to better understand those issues.

For the 2012 Super Bowl, for example, Indianapolis enlisted social media to help it host half a million people in its downtown. These visitors produced a record number of tickets, trash, parking, police issues, and other questions of and demands on city services. But Indianapolis's service had never been better or its response rate higher. Part of the reason was that a dozen college students monitored social media about the Super Bowl, watching for key words in specific places that indicated possible impending problems; they also tweeted in real time to answer questions or direct resources to the right place. It was a hint of what might come with digital governance: by monitoring social media for the first signs of a need, Indianapolis was able to respond even before anyone made a formal request to the government for help.

What makes social networking such a powerful tool for governance? We believe there are five key reasons. First, social media lets people "meet" at their convenience rather than having to be present at a particular time in a particular place. Second, these media allow a wider range of people to participate—not everyone is comfortable speaking to a crowd, but vastly more citizens are accustomed to using a smartphone. Third, social media inherently nudges people to interact with one another and pursue the matter that brought them together. Fourth, social media can weigh in early and often in a decision process, starting sometimes even before a problem has been formally defined. Finally, social media contacts are an easy basis for assembling in-person meetings when those are necessary.

As these examples illustrate, digital governance liberates cities from the notion that government is the source of all reliable information or the solution to every problem. As we will discuss further in chapter 4, we believe city hall should work as a platform to connect communities to each other, giving residents a way to partner with neighbors to prevent some problems and solve others. In the future, advanced systems might even combine official information with data supplied by residents acting as sensors through the various ways they might collect and transmit information. For instance, a road-closing notice could be automatically packaged with tweets or Waze posts about alternate routes gathered from the public in real time.

Even before it began current efforts to redesign its contact center, New York City engaged a subcontractor to provide text services to its 311 call center. Residents could text in a question and receive a texted response from the provider, whose workers selected from an array of official scripts. Although the scripts were frequently updated, the company's workers soon noticed that they could find more up-to-date information about an emerging situation from bloggers than the city was giving them in the posted answers. The company's CEO soon wanted to know if his employees could give out the more up-to-date information instead of the city's responses. In this instance, New York City's government decided the company had to stick to official scripts (because that was the only way to ensure quality, it asserted). The issue, though, will not go away: as more of life becomes digitally enhanced, information about urban problems will increasingly come from a mix of government, private enterprise, and social media. Citizens, of course, will not care where the data comes from.

During one of the small community meetings we have described, Goldsmith heard a Brooklyn businessman who owned a small parking lot complain about the illogic of the city's bicycle parking requirements. The new regulations forced him to give up critical spaces for cars and resulting revenue to serve a need that never manifested itself. He had a much better way to accommodate a cyclist if one ever wanted to use his lot. The city official who wrote the bike parking ordinance never could have anticipated this particular application, because there had not been any effective, easy means for the businessman to communicate with the regulator at an earlier stage when the information might have had an impact. As a result of that meeting, New York City developed a website where agencies list the problems they are trying to solve before announcing the proposed regulations. That's another way in which digital governance encourages meaningful partnerships between citizens and government: these tools eliminate the obstacles that once kept the regulator, the regulated, and the consumer out of contact with each other.

A Personalized and Useful Response

Digital engagement, as we hope we have shown, can do wonders for civic life. But a government that simply responds to engaged digital citizens may inadvertently invest too many resources in the most engaged or the most digital. Data-based governance must thus find ways to guarantee that it serves a broader public. As Harvard lecturer Nicco Mele (previously Howard Dean's digital guru) says, the issue is, "Can you execute policy according to a coherent vision, and can you remain responsive to the people who elected you, when you've got a seemingly endless stream of communications coming at you?"[7] That is the challenge of turning the democratization of data into the creation of meaningful civic voices—voices that represent true communities and achieve true results, and thus foster attachment to community.

Digital governance must create signposts for response and manage customer relations. In its first ten months, Washington's Grade.DC took in over seventy-seven hundred reviews of city services by residents from both online surveys and comments mined from Twitter and other social media. The monthly grades of customer satisfaction are public. More important, the city makes it clear that it responds to these voices. For example, as we mentioned in chapter 2, it moved some DMV staffers away from dealing with the public, and the *Washington Post* reported that when "enough people evaluating the Office on Aging criticized one particular meal ... the chef took it off the rotating menu."[8]

Digital access alone will not change the fact that those with the fewest resources have the weakest voice. City leaders and nonprofits alike need to intentionally facilitate responses from the underserved. Textizen, a Philadelphia-based start-up, supported by the important efforts of Code for America, uses digital, SMS-based tools to reach out to those whose voices often get lost in public decisions affecting their communities. For example, the Philadelphia City Planning Commission partnered with Textizen to reach people who do not attend community meetings. As digital governance expands across cities, we see much opportunity for further work to incorporate the voice of those often ignored. Smartphone use, which is now quite high, even in less affluent neighborhoods, affords the means to gather reactions to city or community services. Adolescents in publicly sponsored after-school programs could be encouraged to use social media to provide reactions and criticisms, for instance. Then, too, why not ask applicants to workforce programs to grade the training on relevance and effectiveness or to share their experiences with other prospective users? To create a better balance between the struggling citizen and his or her services, government or an intermediary can capture, analyze, visualize, and share such data with the community and the potential user of the service.

Real-Time Decision Making

Digital governance also helps cities solve another serious problem—lack of time. As Alfred Tat-Kei Ho wrote in "Reinventing Local Governments and the E-Government Initiative," "A major obstacle to the reinventing government reform is the burden of transaction costs imposed on public officials and citizens. Government officials may find citizen engagement time consuming and costly. Given the time pressure they already face ... public input may seem an unnecessary and unwanted burden."[9] Digital tools supplement community meetings with social media, and paper reports informed by sensor and digital media collected in real time can transform responsiveness. We expect that machine-organized and -curated responses will dramatically reduce the transaction costs of gathering data and organizing feedback almost to zero.

As a deputy mayor, Goldsmith saw large-scale gathering and organization of useful information play out in front of large monitors in a control room at New York City's Department of Transportation. The monitors visualized a steady flow of traffic information coming from GPS devices in individual cars—taxis, which had the transponders in their meters, and private vehicles, whose owners paid their tolls with a device called an E-ZPass that could be read at other locations. Miles away from the control room, in the busiest areas of Midtown Manhattan, traffic lights altered their timing and vehicles moved faster because New York had benefited from anonymous data gathered from different kinds of devices. The city had baked responsiveness into its business processes. This effort, dubbed "Midtown in Motion," contrasts sharply with that of an older analog system where drivers make complaints and the department investigates or studies the problem, and eventually the city does or does not respond.

. . . .

Government, which does not possess enough in terms of resources or force to solve all problems, can use digital governance tools to engage citizens to codesign, coproduce, and codeliver services. Though the digital governance revolution is still young, we can already see the outlines of the platform that cities will provide for engaged citizens. It facilitates personalized and efficient responses, which encourage citizens to participate as members of the community rather than just as consumers collecting their share of services. By participating, residents feel they are bettering their community, building strong networks, and creating change from the ground up. Municipal governments now can establish mechanisms that allow citizens to communicate complaints and solutions easily and effectively. All of these elements build trust in government and trust in one's own capacity as a citizen—the two are mutually reinforcing.

This relationship of trust will be deepened even more when each resident can personalize his or her own city hall. The new contact center platforms we have described will allow constituents to register for notices tailored to their life and community—notices that tell when the nearest softball fields will be available, or when the sidewalk will be repaired, or when parking restrictions near the corner will be lifted. The combination of a personalized city hall combined with facilitated connections to other citizens will create a transformative means of community action and enhanced trust.

When the digital governance revolution is complete, city hall will be completely transformed. Residents will go there (virtually, of course) to register for personalized information (about my school, my park, my corner). And when they get that information, they will automatically know about others in the community who care about the issue and be offered tools to help plan community actions in partnership with government. Government will allow its resources—trucks, planning capacity, labor—to be assigned to participate. Regulators will be able to assess businesses' information in an instant and fast-track businesses with impeccable reputations. Planners will involve communities earlier and more seriously in the decisions that affect them. Budget allocations and priorities will be driven in part by the public—not as a formality but in a genuinely open and sustained process. Bureaucrats will be complimented, and criticized, in real time by an engaged public that will no longer tolerate substandard treatment by its officials. And digital public relations officers will be assigned not just to send out messages about government triumphs, but also to make sure that inbound messages are curated and used to help manage government services. There are no technological barriers left to these vast improvements in urban governance and urban life. The only obstacles are posed by lack of imagination caused by the organization of government, and sometimes by lack of imagination and leadership.

| The City as Digital Platform

Mayor Rahm Emanuel didn't wait long after his inauguration to open Chicago's data to the world. He announced that it would be a priority at his first cabinet meeting in 2011, telling the heads of all departments to "get in line." That set the tone. Those who would use data to improve the lives of Chicagoans would not have to work under cover. The mayor would sweep aside all obstacles.

Less than three years after that meeting, under Mayor Emanuel's strong leadership, Chicago has made itself a distinctly and uniquely digital city—a place where information technology has moved to the policy table. The Mayor's Open Data initiative is only one example of a broad range of developments. To improve scores in city schools and spur economic development, the city is widening the reach of high-speed Internet access infrastructure. To improve government services and engagement with the public, the city has opened its data for use as raw material by developers outside government and policymakers inside city hall. To revolutionize its city planning process, it is using digital tools to plan the design of a new neighborhood to be built on the site of a long-abandoned steel plant. Then, too, Chicago is realizing the decade-old dream of the "smart city." Widespread sensors around the city will soon gather immense amounts of data that will be used to aid research. And the city government no longer simply offers some digital services. It now offers the tools citizens need to write their own apps.

. . . .

In 2010, the technology visionary and O'Reilly Media founder Tim O'Reilly suggested that the digital age would force governments to do more than provide data platforms. Eventually, he said, government would itself be the platform, like the screen display on an iPhone or a tablet—a multipurpose interface on which citizens could rely and for which they would find their own creative new uses. It's an ideal of technology so well integrated into urban life that any citizen can dive deep into data about crime; where anyone can write an app for fellow residents; where data and analytics are built into the work of government to the benefit of all its constituents. It's Chicago, that gruff epitome of an industrial-age metropolis, that is making the city-as-platform idea into reality—joining London, Barcelona, and other global cities in this endeavor.

One morning, on an L platform as he was heading to work, John Tolva met Emanuel as he campaigned for mayor (promising, among other things, to open up Chicago's data to its citizens). At IBM, Tolva had been the company's director of citizenship and technology, responsible for developing socially responsive projects in partnership with nonprofits and governments around the world. He had a strong interest in the policy implications of the use of technology. That chance meeting led to a seat on the new mayor's transition team, where Tolva was asked to write the job description for Chicago's new chief technology officer. "I gave them a list of candidates" but didn't include himself, he told *Crain's Chicago Business*.[1] "I never expected to be offered the job. But I couldn't turn it down. I'd spent all this time advising mayors." Mayor Emanuel also brought on Brett Goldstein, an outspoken and determined data scientist who had been critical to building the restaurant reservations platform OpenTable, as Chicago's—and the nation's—first governmental chief data officer. The mayor had a vision: he wanted to bring Chicago into the digital age.

For one thing, the city had a basic connectivity problem. Chicago is the physical link for many large Internet fiber backbones that run from New York to California. Yet Chicago businesses often can't find reasonably priced fiber Internet access connections for themselves. As of the end of 2012, small businesses in Chicago had to cope with median download speeds of less than 5 mbps and median upload speeds of less than 2 mbps, and medium-size and large businesses were only slightly better off, with a median download speed of less than 17 mbps and a median upload speed of less than 7 mbps. These are paltry numbers, considering that Seoul and Stockholm take 1,000 mbps/1,000 mbps speeds for granted—and pay a fraction of the price for the service that Chicagoans do. The city's private homes are also lagging on Internet access. According to a 2013 study by Karen Mossberger of Arizona State University, about a third of city residents have no Internet connection of any kind at home.[2] These access problems threaten to choke the growth of the high-tech communities that Mayor Emanuel has said the city needs. For a mayor who wants Chicago to be the Seoul of North America, the situation was not acceptable.

And so bringing better high-speed Internet access to Chicago's business community—and eventually its residents—became a top priority for the mayor. At his instigation, the city developed the Mayor's Broadband Challenge, a combination of initiatives aimed at addressing the city's public and private broadband needs. One of those initiatives is running very high-capacity fiber-optic cables through the city's sewers, which is much cheaper and faster than ripping up city streets.

The Mayor's Broadband Challenge is still in early stages. It will bring very-high-capacity connectivity to Chicago businesses at lower prices. It will also have a payoff for the average citizen. With greater high-speed Internet access capacity running through buildings, wireless providers will be able to take advantage of cell towers that have higher-capacity backhaul connections—lines running from the towers to big Internet access cables—to handle calls in the city, much improving cell service.

Beyond the city's downtown, improving access for citizens will require hard-wiring to schools and libraries that will create clouds of connectivity around them that will improve the number and quality of Wi-Fi networks, John Tolva says. If the fiber-optics are for business, the Wi-Fi, Tolva says, will be for school kids. It is part of a long-term plan to improve education in the city. "This isn't about hipsters in cafés," he says. "This is about a kid not having to walk away from his home to the library on a dark night to do his homework."

The expansion of Internet access connectivity, in other words, is a long game: even as it improves the competitiveness of Chicago's workers today, it develops skills and improves educational opportunities for those who will be workers tomorrow. Ultimately the Mayor's Broadband Challenge is all about economic development.

The mayor's message is being amplified by the work of others outside city hall. For example, the Smart Communities initiative, led by the Local Initiative Support Corporation Chicago (LISC Chicago) in conjunction with the city and a dozen community nonprofits, brings digital education, increased Internet access, small business training, digital jobs for youth, and local content portals to five digitally underserved neighborhoods in the Chicago area: Humboldt Park, Pilsen, Englewood, Chicago Lawn, and Auburn Gresham.

Smart Communities began with the City of Chicago's Digital Excellence Initiative, launched by Mayor Daley in 2009 to address Chicago's digital divide. LISC Chicago developed and piloted this neighborhood-based model as a concrete implementation of Mayor Daley's vision with funding from the MacArthur Foundation, the Chicago Community Trust, and the Illinois Department of Commerce and Economic Opportunity. Later, a federal Broadband Technology Opportunities Program grant of seven million dollars allowed Smart Communities to launch programming and intensify efforts in the five neighborhoods. Susana Vasquez, executive director of LISC Chicago, emphasizes that this work is accomplishing much more than simply putting computers in a public space. It is instead a comprehensive approach to making technology relevant to communities. She notes, "What we really pushed first was changing local leaders' mind-sets about the power of technology to help advance community issues, not technology first. If your issues are about safety and poor schools and getting a job, you don't think about technology first. If you start with neighborhood strategy—How do we reduce violence, make it safer to wait for a bus, or improve our schools?—you spark the imagination and motivation of the community leadership and partners."

Funding from the MacArthur Foundation enabled a comprehensive evaluation that proved the effectiveness of this model. Karen Mossberger, Caroline Tolbert, and Chris Anderson analyzed neighborhood-level data for Chicago from 2008 to 2013 and found that the five Smart Communities had experienced significantly higher increases in Internet use, home broadband adoption, and use of the Internet for job, health, and transit searching than other comparable neighborhoods.[3]

Terry Mazany, president and CEO of the Chicago Community Trust (one of the funders of Smart Communities), praised the collaborative approach of this project in that it "builds on the strengths of our civic ecosystem—with public, corporate, nonprofit, and philanthropic sectors all pulling together—to ensure that new information and technology benefit all residents, especially those who lack basic Internet access."

This kind of digital outreach and training, coupled with additional fiber and wireless connectivity in its existing street grid, is just part of Chicago's digital upgrade. Under Mayor Emanuel's sponsorship, the city also plans to add four hundred non-privacy-invasive Internet-connected sensors in secure, boxed locations across the city. That will allow researchers, from academia or the government, to explore the city using data about heat, light, noise, and movement drawn from this rich new source. You can think of those four hundred boxes—designed by the Art Institute of Chicago—as something that a researcher can interrogate or query in the way that people look at weather stations. Use of these boxes will help the city design better-informed policies.

As an example, consider the urban heat island effect. Cities are usually warmer than nearby, less-built-up areas, and the health consequences can be serious: big-city residents suffer more, and die more, in heat waves. Governments want to have an effective response. But urban heat islands are not citywide phenomena. Because of the shade that particular buildings provide, heat islands are block-by-block issues. Hundreds of sensors noting block-by-block variations in temperature could help provide the granular data needed. "This plan is a strong demonstration of the mayor's commitment to opening up Chicago as an urban laboratory," says Brenna Berman, who succeeded Goldstein. "He wants Chicago to be the friendliest city for researchers and companies to come and test their solutions to urban problems."

Indeed, hyperlocal urban sensing, performed by devices in secure networked locations, could transform day-to-day life in a big city. For example, there are four thousand "DivvyBikes" in Chicago's version of the bicycle-sharing system now popular in many large cities. Each of those bikes is equipped with GPS; each could also carry a sensor to pick up what the bike is "feeling" throughout the day. Are its surroundings noisy, crowded, hot, damp, quiet? Such finely grained information could guide policy decisions about traffic management, street furniture, parking rules, and other issues. And apps could be built that would allow users sitting on a city bus to know whether a DivvyBike is available at the next bus stop.

Of course, cities have had networked sensors in neighborhoods for some time now. We know them as surveillance cameras, and all the concerns those cameras have prompted about privacy will certainly come up again as cities add information-gathering devices to more and more everyday public objects. Balancing those concerns against the benefits of sensor technology will be a difficult process, which we expect will continue for many years to come. Chicago has promised that its sensors will respect individual privacy by collecting anonymized info, but the devil is in the details as many different stakeholders wrestle with this tricky problem. All that is certain today is that it will need to be resolved if the digital dream of a responsive city is to reach its full potential.

Another goal of the city-as-platform advocates is to increase and improve the city government's engagement with its constituents. Chicago benefits from a dramatic change in attitudes toward digital civic innovation—a change that is coming from outside city hall. Goldstein, in particular, instilled in an extensive group of outside developers a sense of mission and loyalty—and put them to work. "I knew I needed help, and I wanted to get the community involved and excited about the new day in Chicago," he says. He had a following, and the result was new services that have thousands of people engaging with their government in new and satisfying ways. They're using apps like ServiceTracker (another idea of the mayor), which allows Chicagoans to follow the requests they've made of the city in the same way they might track a UPS or FedEx package. Most of these apps are not created by city employees. Instead, they're written by people who are happy to take advantage of city data, now freely available, as their raw material. Each of these new digital creations adds some general economic benefit as well as the particular service it implements: those who are creating the apps are the kinds of businesses and entrepreneurs Chicago wants to attract to build its tech cred and bolster its economic growth.

That said, Chicago's government is determined not to get all its digital input from the obvious candidates. The city wants to communicate more broadly with its traditionally poor neighborhoods. Residents there are now routinely invited to test new apps and websites, and the city hopes they will write their own apps too. After all, the most useful apps will likely be neighborhood specific.

. . . .

Goldstein had spent his first few months as chief data officer housed in the mayor's office. That, he recognizes, gave him an important symbolic and practical boost as he started his work: "It gave me sponsorship, a political buffer, and autonomy."

With Mayor Emanuel determined to fulfill his campaign promise to open Chicago's data, Goldstein knew what he had to do. Urban data didn't faze him. He'd worked with this data for years, first while getting his master's degree in criminal justice and then while building the Chicago Police Department's first Predictive Analytics Group within the Counterterrorism and Intelligence Section, where he worked on models to predict crime. It was the "open" part of the plan that was new and, with his counterterrorism experience, against his instincts at first. But Goldstein proved to be a quick learner.

Four months into his new job, in September 2011, Goldstein had all incident-level crime data for the city, back to 2001, released online—almost five million records, which automatically updated to stay current. It was the largest such set of incident-level crime data ever released. By then, the city had already made city contracts and lobbying data available on data.cityofchicago.org. Goldstein had based that site on a platform sold by Socrata, the Seattle-based company dedicated to getting government data to the public. "It's a whole new era of openness and transparency," Goldstein told the *Chicago Tribune* at the time. "You determine your own analysis."[4]

At the start of Emanuel's administration earlier that year, Chicago had been releasing significantly less data to the public than other cities. Now, with Goldstein working away, Chicago had one of the biggest open data programs in the United States, with almost five hundred datasets providing regularly updated raw, machine-readable data. Today the city's online data portal allows the public (and, of course, the media) to view data in the form of charts, maps, and calendars. Those user-friendly views make Chicago's site more practically open than many other portals: the data is not just online, but online in usable, understandable formats. Goldstein was making the city-as-platform vision more real with each passing day. When he wasn't writing apps, he was providing hooks and gateways into publicly held data so that other people could write the software.

Civic app development has been thriving in Chicago ever since. For example, thanks to publicly available data from the Chicago Transit Authority and Chicago's Application Programming Interface for working with that information, commuters now have their pick of time-saving mobile apps. With names like Buster and QuickTrain, these apps combine GPS data from users' phones with transit information—and tell users where exactly a desired bus or train is and how to get to the closest stop or station where they can catch it. There are never enough app developers in city government, and so a key city role is to publish data.

Having open data was just a first step for Goldstein. He still had his youthful enthusiasm for wielding data against violence, so he wanted to apply predictive analytics—the use of past data to forecast future developments—to solve, or prevent, other urban problems. He decided to produce a real analytic product every sixty to ninety days. "I didn't want to [just] make long-term promises," he says. "I wanted to produce something real."

One of Goldstein's favorite success stories in this area arose from Mayor Emanuel's concerns about "food deserts"—stretches of the city where it's hard to buy fresh, affordable, and healthy food. About 70 percent of people who live in Chicago's food deserts are African American, and most of the deserts are on Chicago's South and West Sides. Only a month into his tenure as mayor, at a food desert summit he had convened, Mayor Emanuel showed maps indicating where new supermarkets were both necessary and economically viable. Goldstein had found a way to take data locked up in spreadsheets or lists and visualize the information on the kind of street map with which any city dweller is comfortable. That allowed the information to be displayed in a way Chicagoans could immediately understand—connected to buildings and streets rather than featureless strings of 1s and 0s. Giving people a view rather than a list makes it possible for them to act on information far more quickly.

Robert Scoble and Shel Israel in *The Age of Context* identify the five forces driving technological innovation today: mobile, social media, data, sensors, and location. Chicago uses location to provide context for the other four. As Goldstein says, "The value of such maps goes far beyond making the issues understandable."[5] Mapped data can supply arguments for or against a particular policy, because they give real-time information in the place of dated theories. "If you think a policy move makes sense," he says, "and all you have is old journal articles [to support it], we need to have more on that." One of the less visible but important consequences of digital governance, he says, is that it makes policymakers accustomed to the idea that their ideas must be supported by relevant information. When policies were being considered during his time in city hall, he says proudly, "If I said data wasn't there, things stopped." Confidence in the data let him take the risk of saying no to powerful constituencies, including his boss: "My commitment to [Mayor] Rahm [Emanuel] was that I'd do what is right, and if he needed to fire me, that's fine."

. . . .

Goldstein never got fired, but he often lost patience with the slow workings of traditional government. Rather than wait for meetings and approvals, he frequently found it easier to go to his office, close the door, and do the coding work that pried data out of existing databases and brought it into Chicago's public data portal. That was how both the crime data release and the food desert project were done so quickly. What was important was to keep up the pace of change: the more data was released, the more people could learn from and use it, and the more the city as a whole would learn about facts once kept to one walled-in part of the government or another.

To help him, Goldstein assembled a team from a variety of sources. Some were policy associates whom the mayor's office had brought in. Some were in the government's IT department. Some were the people Goldstein called the NerdHerd: volunteers from Chicago's tech community whom he had inspired and recruited early in his tenure. NerdHerd members trained city employees and citizens in the ways of open databases and made many other ingenious, invaluable contributions. One, for example, developed an automated way to assess tweets about the transit system to find the ones that were complaints.

Goldstein's long-term goal is a data system that makes Chicago's city government a little more like Amazon or Google: an enterprise that routinely uses large amounts of real-time data to predict future outcomes and adjusts nimbly as circumstances change. With different city departments' data combined to show relationships among events that seemed to have nothing to do with each other, the city could understand itself differently. With predictive analytics, the city government could even actively prevent future harms instead of merely reacting after the fact. This is Goldstein's vision: the city as smart data platform.

In any city hall, though, visions of a great future must compete with immediate problems, for which data has to be mustered right here, right now. In early 2012, for instance, Chicago's new government knew it had to plan for a major disruptive event: a NATO summit meeting scheduled for May 2012. The situation was unprecedented. This would be the first North American NATO meeting not held in Washington, DC, and it would require the city to coordinate its responses with federal and state officials, as well as representatives of scores of nongovernmental organizations. And all this would have to happen in the face of mass protests.

To handle the challenges, the city's chief operating officer, Lisa Schrader (who later became the mayor's chief of staff), wanted to be able to look deep into the data on any particular area of Chicago she chose. She wanted to be able to see right away what assets (like fire hydrants) the city had in that neighborhood, as well as its record of 911 and 311 service calls, public safety information, tweets emanating from the area, and other useful information. Goldstein was put on the case in the fall of 2011 to create all the digital tools Schrader wanted. The problem wasn't just that time was short; it was also that there was nothing in the marketplace that could do what Schrader wanted. She needed a tool that would pull multiple types of data from disparate systems and assemble the information into a visual presentation that would tell her all she needed to know about any given situation.

Goldstein soon joined up with Danielle DuMerer, a project manager and kindred spirit he had identified in the Department of Innovation and Technology. To save time and money, the pair (along with dozens of others) built a system using applications that Chicago already had on the shelf. For example, to present the needed shared data within a map interface, Goldstein used the city's existing license to Esri's Geographic Information System (GIS) mapping application. To manage the data that fed the system, Goldstein and DuMerer used MongoDB, an open source database product.

The result, called WindyGrid, worked for Schrader. It also served the mayor's long-term digital vision. As the first product Chicago built on a foundation of data that crossed departmental boundaries, it proved just how helpful that kind of data sharing could be. Thanks to WindyGrid, all agencies and organizations involved in the city's handling of the NATO summit could see the impacts of their decisions and make quick adjustments. Even more impressive, the entire project had cost only about one hundred thousand dollars. The NATO summit is receding into history, but WindyGrid endures, offering a unified look at city operations to any department that needs it.

. . . .

In June 2012, Goldstein moved out of the mayor's office to become the city's chief information officer and commissioner of the city's Department of Innovation and Technology (DoIT), and Berman became first deputy commissioner (she later succeeded Goldstein in the CIO job in 2013). From now on, DoIT, not the mayor's suite, would be the official home of Chicago's data analytics, open data, and other data functions. This allowed the team to get bigger and protected it from political cross-winds, says Berman, who had been one of city hall's deputy budget directors focused on enterprise initiatives and performance management. Berman, who worked with Goldstein on many digital projects, remembers that the idea was to give her and Goldstein the scope to remake the city's entire approach to technology and innovation—an ambition of the mayor they were well prepared to realize given Berman's background in management consulting and business operations at IBM and Goldstein's grounding in tech. Their plan was to get beyond the pilot stage by embedding technology in everything the city did in order to drive decision making. "We wanted to help all of our departments turn their data into valuable information to make decisions," Berman says. Under the pair's leadership, DoIT was renovated to become a modern innovative hub: overall information technology operations were greatly improved across the city, and predictive analytics are being embedded in every agency operation.

The next structural step was to institutionalize open data policies so that each of Chicago's thirty agencies would help advance the work rather than wait for instructions from on high. In December 2012, Mayor Emanuel issued an executive order requiring each department to designate an open data coordinator, responsible for contributing usable public data to the open data portal. The coordinator would also be responsible for the accuracy of the data. And DoIT would be required to produce a biannual report documenting the city's progress on open data and transparency. It was a remarkable step toward making digital governance business as usual. Ultimately each of these designated people will be responsible for using and improving WindyGrid and analyzing data for his or her department as well. This structural change ensures that Chicago's commitment to open data and transparency, as well as analytics, will live beyond Mayor Emanuel's time in office.

. . . .

Berman has begun Chicago's next transformational digital step forward by initiating the creation of the SmartData platform, an open-source predictive analytics application that will allow all thirty city agencies to query data without the aid of a professional data engineer. To make that vision a reality, Berman's enthusiasm and decade of experience helping governments adopt complex analytics programs will be useful to her as she persuades city departments that using predictive analytics—analyzing millions of lines of data in real time so as to detect relationships—will help agencies make smarter, earlier decisions that address a wide range of urban challenges. (This persuasion task is probably more difficult than any technological issues that may come up.) Berman has been doing her political work slowly and carefully. In each city department, she says, the DoIT is looking for "a single use case to prove to the leadership [that] this is important to them." Agencies generate these use cases together with DoIT by identifying their biggest business challenges, defining those that are most susceptible to a predictive approach, and then addressing those issues in newly effective ways. That's what will motivate departments to use the platform.

As an example of a successful use case, she often talks about rats. Berman learned about the rat issue when she and her staff were looking at 311 data for variables that were affecting each other. Her team "noticed that certain variables were pointing toward changes in the number of rodent calls." Berman's team doesn't try to engage a department until it has something compelling. This seemed to fit the bill. So the team sat down with deputy commissioners in the Department of Streets and Sanitation and the commissioner, Charlie Williams.

The sell was very soft. "We've been playing with your 311 data and we found a couple of interesting things," they said. That's because Berman knows that "nothing offends an expert more than pretending you know their job better than they do." Treading carefully, she finds, leaves space for the experts to notice that a predictive model can be their friend. Often, in fact, the model aligns with the expert's own intuitions.

The rat team within Streets and Sanitation was run by Josie Cruz, a long-time city employee who cares deeply about her work and was happy to collaborate with Berman's team. She wanted to know all about the thirty-one types of 311 calls that appeared to correlate with subsequent rat trouble in an area. Some of those correlations confirmed Cruz's intuition, such as the rat complaints that she noticed had often been preceded by 311 calls about dead birds.

Berman's team showed Cruz data about how her Streets and Sanitation Rodent Control unit had been doing its work on rats, mapped against DoIT's predictions of how it could work based on its analysis. The overlap was 80 percent; most of the locations DoIT would have suggested going to, based on the data, were locations Cruz also would have targeted. Cruz was fascinated. From Berman's perspective, it was a perfect use case—one that "prove[s] out with the data what the team is already doing based on their expertise."

Berman wants one such case for each department, because DoIT wants those departments "to be comfortable. We want them to trust us. We want to build that relationship," she says. Like Mike Flowers of New York City's Office of Data Analytics, profiled in chapter 6, Berman wants the city agencies to be on board with data analytics. That's one reason she chose rats. Streets and Sanitation is also responsible for snow removal, trash pickup, and tree trimming, but DoIT wasn't going near those political hotspots. "While rats are sort of gross and you don't want to get that call, it's not the city's most risky service," she says.

Thus, using historical water, street, sanitation, and rodent data, DoIT was able to build a model to help it decide whether and where the city should be putting out rat bait. Was it worth it? It turned out it was. "Nobody loves talking about rodent problems, but when you're a city that is on a large lake, it's something you take very seriously, and we can actually make rodent baiting more efficient and effective if we do it proactively [rather] than wait for the problem to occur," Berman says.

As always, executive leadership was a key element of getting an agency to adopt the data analytics approach. Streets and Sanitation commissioner Williams, who might have been suspicious of a technical gizmo telling him how to do his job, supported the data team. Williams, who builds PCs as a hobby in his basement, was open to the facts. Once he could see there was a proper pilot and could see the numbers for himself, he was fully onboard.

In fact, in picking the initial case for each department, Berman follows a checklist in deciding whether a particular departmental data analytics use case is worth pursuing by her team. Rodent control met many of the checklist's elements. The proposed case has to solve a business problem that the department really cares about—check. It can't be too politically difficult—check (rats, as Berman notes, have zero political support). Implementing the analytical approach can't be too difficult for city workers—check (Cruz was already watching 311 call data in order to decide how to react. To benefit from the model, all she had to do was add some different types of calls to those she monitored).

So Berman and Williams decided to go ahead with a beautifully structured pilot project that was designed with the assistance of computer scientists from Carnegie Mellon University who had been involved with Chicago's data work since Goldstein was with the Chicago Police Department. They set up four dedicated rodent control teams, each alternating its methods for a week. One week they would use the DoIT's filter, based on its analytics, to target rat baiting. The next week, they'd go about their jobs the usual way. In the first week of the pilot, a rodent control team was directed by the DoIT filter to a house that hadn't even been the subject of a 311 call about rats. That place turned out to have the largest infestation the Chicago Department of Streets and Sanitation had ever seen. The pilot was looking to be an enormous win for the data team.

But then Berman got a call from the mayor's operating team: there was some confusion about what was going on. It turned out that one of the thirty-one call types that predicts the presence of rats is one in which a resident asks the city to pick up and replace one of the black trash carts it issues free to households. The Department of Streets and Sanitation has a big backlog of these black-cart pickup requests. Someone on the mayor's operating team had gotten the idea that if Josie Cruz's pilot kept going, the department would get more and more calls for black carts because citizens would think a dilapidated cart was related to rat problems. "And the backlog would get bigger and the department would fall behind on their performance metrics even further," Berman says. Another lesson learned: DoIT has to help people understand analytics.

Berman called a meeting and clearly explained that black-cart calls were just one variable among many. But the reaction of the mayor's operating team reflected one of the most important lessons to be learned from Chicago's experience: leadership must come from the top but has to be delivered in the form of empowerment. The insights that would come out of these pilots depended on collaborative problem solving. The city would operate better if the planning process for these pilots included the mayor's office.

. . . .

City hall understood that the benefits of this effort exceeded the downsides and that the project as a whole would set the stage for many more breakthroughs. And so the SmartData platform keeps growing, one use case at a time. Berman plans to meet with every commissioner in every key Chicago department during this start-up phase, to take them through a description of what the platform is, how the city will be using it, and how participation in it will help every department. She will be asking the departments about the problems they'd like to solve. She will run workshops with groups of departments so as to encourage them to think about possibilities for cross-agency synergies. She will look for use cases that are interesting to the mayor and other constituencies.

Berman hopes to create a platform that is user-friendly for nonengineers. She is careful about the sensitive subject of police and other public safety data. The police, she notes, "have their own analytics staff." She knows the next three years will include working with police staff to align their analytics plans with those of other agencies.

If all this work goes well, Chicago will have a SmartData platform that will be widely useful—helping many city governments to become more responsive. It will be made of freely available open-source code, allowing every city to use the parts of which the platform is made (and to use any data and algorithms Chicago chooses to make available to the outside world). Former New York City mayor Michael Bloomberg's foundation has given Chicago one million dollars to make this dream come true. As we said in chapter 3 when we described Joe Morrisroe's work in New York City, Berman's vision for the new Chicago SmartData platform will create a tool set that other cities can reuse with no start-up software development costs. The technology team in Chicago is also creating an archive of instructive documents and templates that will give other cities a road map for developing their own predictive analytics projects, enabling collaborative solutions.

If such a city-as-platform can be created and then replicated around the world, cities would be able to interrogate each others' data directly and easily. The benefits could be enormous: city governments would be able to learn from one another with enormous speed and efficiency. It would lower the barriers created by siloed agency operations, as city halls around the world no longer answered basic urban governance questions—How do I best target emergency services during dangerous weather? How do I target health service interventions so that they will have the greatest impact?—in isolation. Since 2012, Chicago has been migrating its disparate sources of public data into a data warehouse that will someday feed the SmartData platform; other cities could soon be doing the same.

. . . .

As valuable to a city government as predictive power is the ability to learn from normalized data across cities. In support of this multicity data vision, Chicago has released the Data Dictionary, a first-of-its kind metadata repository that serves as a central catalogue of descriptive information for all of Chicago's datasets and databases. For each dataset, the Data Dictionary contains information such as the owner's contact information, date of update, and descriptions of the kinds of data it contains. It was built with support from the MacArthur Foundation in a partnership between the city and Chapin Hall at the University of Chicago, a research and policy center. Chicago's director of analytics and performance, Tom Schenk Jr., noted how critical these partners were to the dictionary's development, saying, "We've been able to add innovation into the technology sphere by leveraging these partnerships."

The Data Dictionary is a model project for cities, and because it was built on an open source platform, other cities can adapt it for their own purposes. Chicago has already begun conversations with other cities hoping to build their own Data Dictionary. According to Schenk, "The Data Dictionary's functionality is becoming absolutely crucial but not something that is being looked at enough. As we become more data-oriented and it's becoming easier and cheaper to collect more data, how do you know where and what it is? So collecting and being able to search metadata is becoming almost if not more important as access." In other words, although Chicago is not releasing all of its data, it is revealing all the different kinds of data it has. This makes it possible for other cities to understand Chicago's data resources and even in the future to connect with them. It is, the Chicago team hopes, the beginning of the digital governance equivalent of railroad-gauge standardization: the replacement of idiosyncratic and incompatible structures with forms that are shared by all and used by all. This effort, with its enormous generative implications, may be Chicago's—and Mayor Emanuel's—biggest contribution to the responsive city movement.

Dan O'Neil, whom we met in chapter 2, runs the CUT (Civic User Testing) Group that check Chicago's apps before they are released. It's part of his work at the Smart Chicago Collaborative, an indispensable part of the civic tech story in Chicago. O'Neil and his group take city hall's digital inventions into neighborhoods to see if they will fly in the real world. Often, they find, data and applications mean very different things at street level than they did at city hall.

For example, Smart Chicago played a crucial role in field-testing schoolcuts.org, a website designed by the mayor's office to help parents understand what schools were being closed and why. O'Neil took the idea to his CUT Group, present in every one of the city's fifty wards. The CUT Group, Tolva says, are "a way of trying to break out of the downtown, city hall mentality [that says], 'Oh, yeah, this will be useful.'" For schoolcuts.org, O'Neil gave each participant a five-dollar gift card to try out the interface. They hated it. Parents could not understand the data being used. For that matter, many couldn't understand the app at all: it was not presented in their native languages. Result: the app was changed.

For the long term, the people participating in community user testing groups will be useful in helping the city figure out how to balance surveillance with privacy; the only way the city will learn the location of the dividing line between "I feel like this is helping my city" and "This creeps me out" will be to test things with its residents. Smart Chicago Collaborative's motto is, "If it doesn't work for you, it doesn't work."

Smart Chicago Collaborative has already helped city hall avoid some political scrapes. When the mayor's office was thinking about releasing the city's Open311 interface, it realized that for the first time in city history, its fifty aldermen would be able to see the status of service requests in the other wards. They had always been able to see the requests in their own locations, and now they'd have visibility into everyone else's. That was a big deal: they'd be able to see whether services were being distributed equitably. Clearly this was fraught with lots of political implications, and yet this information needed to be visible. How could the city get this done without annoying the aldermen? "And so," says John Tolva, "Smart Chicago Collaborative built that—it's called ChicagoWorksForYou.com." The mayor's office avoided heat for building an interface that might reveal some uncomfortable facts by pointing over to Smart Chicago. Its easily usable interface, and inarguable data, calmed the waters; Smart Chicago provided the technical smarts to make this possible.

City officials often worry whether opening their data to the public will embarrass their administrations. The reality is almost always the opposite. People who want to embarrass or attack city hall can always find ammunition. But concerned residents and interested app developers end up helping city hall when they know more. The ties of trust and democracy are strengthened by openness.

Epilogue: A Platform Built from Scratch

About ten miles south of downtown Chicago, alongside Lake Michigan, sits the colossal former US Steel South Works site. The mills there started churning out steel in 1901; the plant shut down, along with much of the rest of the American steel industry, in the 1990s, and the site has been silent ever since. Now, McCaffery Interests, a real estate development company, is working with architects at Skidmore, Owings & Merrill to develop the tract. What they're planning, together with Tolva, Goldstein, and Charlie Catlett of the University of Chicago's Urban Center for Computation and Data, is a whole new neighborhood. It will be called Lakeside and will be built from scratch to be digitally responsive.

Even now, in its planning phase, the project is using data science in unprecedented ways to make life better for future residents. In a few years, this parcel of land, just south of downtown, could be the smartest neighborhood in Chicago and perhaps the smartest neighborhood in North America.

The master plan for Lakeside includes almost fourteen thousand single-family dwellings and high-rise units, about eighteen million square feet of retail services, more than a hundred acres of parks and bike paths, and a high school. "It's a massive undertaking," says John Tolva. "It's bigger than the Loop."

Lakeside could bring many benefits to its part of Chicago. (For one thing, it would give its neighbors on Chicago's South Side access to Lake Michigan, which they have never had.) But a lot of Tolva's enthusiasm is, of course, digital. McCaffery and Skidmore are using data-driven decision-making tools to plan this enormous project, modeling the impact of the development on the transportation and energy patterns of the surrounding area. Sensible as that may sound, it almost never happens, Tolva says: "Brett [Goldstein] and I were actually using very sophisticated tools to model the management of the city, and yet the people that we employ to build it are not using those tools."

Charlie Catlett and his colleagues at the University of Chicago would like to change that business-as-usual attitude in the building field, and Catlett thinks the Lakeside project could be just the lever that's needed. A gentle-voiced researcher with a deep background in data science, Catlett is helping McCaffery and Skidmore connect changes in zoning, scale, and density to the future Lakeside's energy use and transportation patterns. Catlett has brokered a research agreement between Chicago's Argonne National Labs, where Catlett is a senior computer scientist, and McCaffery, and he's now seeking additional funding from the National Science Foundation. He hopes to use what the planners have already learned to guide energy supply plans and make changes in the building code before work on Lakeside begins.

Catlett's first data tool, LakeSim, has been a hit with staffers at McCaffery and Skidmore. By playing with the sliders and parameters of different settings inside LakeSim, including zoning, construction schedules, and potential changes in climate, the developer and architect can see what effects changes in their plans may have on energy and transportation demand today and, eventually, on air quality, well-being, and a host of other outcomes. LakeSim allows them to experiment with the effects of zoning decisions or projected construction dates for single buildings, over periods of decades. (Despite its name, LakeSim is not SimCity. Limited to real data and positive outcomes, its choices are too constrained to make for a fun game.)

Naturally Catlett hopes this kind of data-informed exploration at the planning stage will foster smart digital governance once Lakeside is built and connected to the rest of Chicago. By predicting the effects of density and design on such urban essentials as transport, air quality, and safety from crime, he notes, the models may be able to address questions that otherwise would require twenty years of bad experience to answer. For example, if the completed Lakeside is dense with the types of urban sensors we have described above, it could provide the basis for positive change in existing practices city-wide and, ultimately, in many other cities. If he could see, minute-by-minute, the patterns in electricity use in a 150,000-person town such as Naperville, Illinois (with its smart grid deployment), Catlett says, "then I could run various models and compare them to see if they would predict the actual behavior of energy use in a city, enabling dynamic energy markets that could offer incentives for clean energy use." That would quickly lead him to a model that matched real life. That model would be useful for more than transportation questions, he notes. "If there's a way to infer whether someone is at home or not from energy use, then you might be able to validate some of the transportation models." Just as important, the framework developed for this project will be publicly available. One reason he is so interested in building a sensor ecosystem is to make sure such data never ends up locked up in a proprietary database.

. . . .

Catlett has lined up both John Tolva and Brett Goldstein as fellows of his Urban Center for Computation and Data at Argonne National Laboratory and the University of Chicago. Tolva is interested in the built environment policy questions for Lakeside; Goldstein, predictably, is interested in data analytics for the site. Catlett thinks that we are just at the beginning of revolutionizing the data analytics process in planning and validation of those plans once made. He is looking for real data collection before an intervention begins—and, here, the "intervention" is

Lakeside itself. Then he wants to pull in planning and validation data from other cities and to be able to present his results to social scientists.

The dream for Catlett is that Lakeside will be a twenty-first-century city in the middle of an existing city. At least, the brand-new digital neighborhood could be a good influence on the rest of the city. But one thing is certain: whether or not Lakeside is built, Chicago will be at the forefront of the digital revolution for a long time to come.

| The Responsive Employee

In 2011, a blizzard of complaints from residents living on Manhattan's Second Avenue fell on the shoulders of Lolita Jackson, then a special projects officer in the New York City Mayor's office. The city's Metropolitan Transportation Authority had stepped up its work on its decades-old plan to build a subway under the avenue, beginning with a mile-and-a-half stretch from 64th to 96th streets. More than seventy years had passed since the last time new subway lines were built in New York, and citizens weren't prepared for or happy about what they had to endure. Noise, debris, and obstructions closed one small shop after another in the construction zone, infuriating residents. So did the sudden lack of parking due to an influx of parked cars owned by workers involved in the construction.

Meanwhile, scaffolding blocked streetlights from illuminating the sidewalk. Garbage trucks looked for trash bags in their usual locations, oblivious to the fact that construction had blocked off those sites, and so they didn't pick up the waste. The actions of city enforcement agents, doing their jobs as required by specific performance criteria, rubbed salt on people's wounds: sanitation officers issued tickets to local businesses for failing to pick up construction workers' garbage, and traffic officers ticketed delivery trucks forced to double-park by the construction.

The city's street-level workers were doing their jobs exactly as required by their work rules—which meant severely limiting their ability to use common sense by taking individual circumstances into account. After a tour of the area, the deputy mayor of operations (Goldsmith) placed Jackson in charge of addressing these problems. She quickly launched into action, naming people to a cross-agency group that walked once a week through affected areas to speak with business owners, observe conditions, and provide immediate help where possible. This group also met weekly at city hall to identify and possibly preempt issues.

As a result of her fact finding, Jackson soon improved trash removal with changed routes and specially built bins. She also changed lighting on the avenue, improved signage around the work sites and worked with the firms building the tunnel to mitigate neighborhood complaints about their employee parking.

Every one of Jackson's solutions increased the trust and patience of the community for the loud, dusty, ongoing construction. That, in turn, had a measurable impact on the quality of life on Second Avenue: business closures in the construction zone plummeted. In the place of what we call wholesale government—one size fits all, one rule applies always—Jackson had delivered a more flexible, personal, retail version of municipal service. Her approach was personal and oriented toward customer satisfaction. She made the resident, not the rule, her priority.

Urban government needs more responsive employees like Lolita Jackson, oriented toward commonsense solutions for real people rather than adherence to a culture of rule-bound government that was new in 1890. One of the reasons we believe that the digital revolution in governance will make such a difference is that it will help find, equip, empower, and even create more public servants like her.

In their extensive research on employees, David E. Bowen and Edward E. Lawler III noticed that performance gains occurred often in two circumstances.[1] One was while taking steps to "recover" from poor service delivery (e.g., relocating a hotel guest from a noisy room to a better one rather than shrugging and saying, "I wish there was something I could do"). The other was while adapting service to meet the particular needs of an individual (e.g., finding a guest a room that overlooks the zoo, even though there is nothing in the rules about that amenity). Mobile information tools facilitate both of these responses. Monitoring tweets, as we have explained, is a powerful way to find out how people are responding to events, which makes it a way to find poor service delivery early enough to correct it. And employees in the field who not only can access all city data about a particular complaint or address but receive suggestions about interventions are in a position to tailor their actions to the individual case before them. We believe that much of the benefit of digital governance will come from the way it frees public employees to replace the crude methods of wholesale government with nimbler and more personalized retail approaches.

When that change is complete, the customer satisfaction that public servants create will be measured in civic participation and trust in government. All of this will increase the responsiveness of the public enterprise as well as help the government become adaptable and less mechanistic. Attention to customer satisfaction by public employees will result in more effective and responsive services, greater civic engagement, and a higher quality of life.

Retail Government

Such is our hope. But of course today retail government and retail merchants seldom resemble each other. Compare the typical citizen's experience of government service with the typical customer experience at Finish Line, a 650-store retailer of athletic shoes (Goldsmith serves on its board).

When a customer enters one of the company's stores, he is met by a sales associate, equipped with a mobile device. Is he a repeat customer? If so, the device provides not only details about inventory but also about the shopper's own preferences, drawn from previous visits to a store or the company's website. (If he is new to the store, those preferences will be recorded for future reference.) The sales associate can then do her best to match color, size, and price to the needs of the shopper. She can even complete the sale on the device in her hand.

If the athletic shoe retailer were run like a typical local government, customers would line up at a counter, where eventually each would fill out a form, reentering the same information given at previous visits. They would then each be offered a gray shoe—often, but not always, in the right size. Anyone who got the wrong size would of course have the right to complain through channels. Each complaint would generate a work order, and eventually a worker would be sent out to investigate.

Such is the legacy of an age of reform that calcified decades ago: public agencies simply have a higher degree of formalization than private firms. The profusion of rules and regulations in government prevents managers from granting street-level employees enough discretion to change the way work is structured and performed.

Government, as we described in the Introduction, remains task oriented instead of results oriented. When the task is defined in advance and does not change, government cannot respond effectively to new information or to the kind of predictive analytics that are becoming routine in other walks of life. No wonder both citizens and public servants end up frustrated by the encounters that they have within this system. Its rigidity and inflexibility create many pain points: the difficulty of making the original request for action; the lack of customized, easily available options; and the complicated process necessary to remediate any hiccup in the delivery of the public service.

If citizens hate this frustrating tangle, so do most employees. Alan Altshuler, who helped form the Innovations in American Government Program at Harvard Kennedy School, has found that responsive innovation is more likely to be made by public employees working at the street level than by managers higher up in the hierarchy of wholesale government.[2] Direct contact with constituents produces both the incentive to innovate and the knowledge required to do so effectively. As state and local government expert Michael Lipsky has noted, in some street-level public occupations, it is essential that decisions are not just made in accordance with preexisting rules but in response to the individual case, by workers who combine a deep knowledge of the field with commitment and a common sense that cannot be codified.[3] But lack of authority, training, and applicable tools often prevents the civil servant from responding as he or she would prefer.

The Newly Successful Public Employee

In most cities, repair supervisors act as overseers: they follow the workers, keeping track of their time and attendance, observing them work, and restricting impromptu acts. All of their observations and evaluations are recorded in voluminous paper-filled files. In Boston, though, workers use more of their own discretion to manage priorities, in coordination with their bosses. That's possible because they receive up-to-the-minute information about the location and severity of service requests on mobile devices from the City Worker app we described in chapter 1. "It changed the way that we do the work," says Matt Mayrl, Boston Public Works Department's Chief of Staff. That workers have more discretion on the job isn't the only advantage of the app. Using it has also made the supervisors more effective, he says. "I don't know any other public works department that has its district supervisors—whose job used to be following behind crews making sure the work was done—who are now around the city on advanced mobile devices creating new or revised assignments, accompanied by online entries of pictures that can be shared with the public." These empowered workers provide better service for constituents.

Permitting without Killing Jobs

Inevitably government faces responsibilities involving conflicting goals—how to ensure health and safety while helping a small business get up and started, for example. Elaborate regulatory processes extract a high price from the legitimate, earnest business or contractor in order to weed out the infrequent, but dangerous, abuser. Such sharp trade-offs are simply no longer necessary.

Permitting, another important service provided by government, could be greatly improved by digital empowerment. Now that we're in the second decade of the twenty-first century, an ideal city permit system (for a building or a new business opening) should contain no paper at all. The technology is readily available: an applicant could file all documents in searchable digital formats. Then every decision and addition by an agency would be made in digital form and, of course, be available to all city employees working on the filing and to the applicant as well. Instead of clerks doing the rote work of checking filled-in boxes and filing forms, a highly trained analyst, assigned to intake, would use analytics to grade the application based on the danger and complexity of the project and on a thorough search concerning all of the principals. This would include an examination of other public databases for any history of previous violations, safety records, compliance with applicable laws, tax delinquencies, and verified claims by customers or employees. Identification-verification software would then confirm the accuracy of the information provided.

Such a scoring system would allow the city to fast-track applicants with good records. Not having to spend time scrutinizing impeccable businesses, city workers could spend more effort examining more complex or questionable applications. Professionally trained reviewers would make better decisions more quickly.

Imagine the difference if a committed city employee working in a park could operate like a Finish Line worker. If, say, a parent asked the public servant to fix a broken seat on the swing set in the playground, she would respond by using her smartphone. She would take a photo of the problem, place an order for its repair, obtain a tracking number and a date for the work to be done, and give that information to the person who had reported the problem. Imagine how the replacement of an opaque and lengthy process with a simple five-minute transaction would affect the attitudes of that citizen and the employee.

As we argue throughout this book, such a transformation is entirely possible. The technology exists, and the thirst for change is quite clear. All that is required, as the stories we have told in this book have shown, are determination and leadership.

Working Smarter: Data-Driven Decision Making

In the literature concerning organizational innovation, practices that share managers' power with employees are clearly correlated with innovation. By loosening controls, managers give entrepreneurial employees freedom to tinker with existing elements and practices and reconfigure them in new ways. Pushing authority downward also encourages employees to find new solutions by imparting a sense of control and responsibility for the quality of their work. Data-driven governance can help on both fronts.

Targeting Social Services with Data

Consider the dilemma of the child welfare office. Over the past few years a number of state and large county directors of child welfare have found themselves vilified in their local media. Many of them have lost their jobs. Given the problems in their jurisdictions, even the best of these directors operate in a difficult "gotcha!" world: they oversee thousands of employees with varying levels of commitment, training, and industriousness, all of whom make difficult decisions about vulnerable children. Federal mandates impose extra costs and burdens, many of them aimed at ensuring that often poorly paid caseworkers comply with rigid procedures. When one of their decisions goes badly wrong and leads to a death, or when a case falls through the cracks, the media and political enemies of the governor descend.

As we said in the Introduction, digital data and communication tools have been helping these highly stressed government agencies do a better job for the fragile families they serve.

Given such limited resources, it is critical for government social service agencies to target their outreach to those who need it most. New York's Department of Homeless Services is collaborating with the SumAll Foundation to identify eviction hotspots with a large number of families requiring assistance. Visualizations of data from current shelter intake processes allow them to identify neighborhoods where many people have been recently evicted, allowing them to pinpoint their services to prevent more residents from becoming homeless. "We are helping social workers microtarget prevention outreach," said Stefan Heeke, executive director of the SumAll Foundation. "They receive a list from us with specific high-risk families for individual outreach and a block-by-block heat map for local outreach. Our analysis makes their efforts much more effective and also buys precious time in the prevention process." This ability to see trends based on data allows homeless-service employees to focus on their ultimate goal of preventing homelessness in the first place rather than providing shelter.

Once a service worker has been matched with the right person in need of services, data can further assist her in finding the best support for a client. In some jurisdictions, technology is allowing a new kind of child welfare caseworker to emerge: one who visits a troubled family with up-to-the-minute and complete data at her fingertips, plus decision-support tools that identify risk factors based on the whole population. It's all available in the tablet she carries in lieu of a file filled with paper.

With a complete data picture of both the individual family and the at-risk population as a whole, the worker, aided by decision support tools powered by analytics, can quickly grasp the situation. She is in a position to ask the right questions and, with discretion informed by digital support, guide the family to the solutions that are likely to work best. This personalized approach isn't just better for the families it serves. By doing a better job of matching constituents to services, it also saves money.

This, we believe, is the future of public service, made possible by digital tools. Where today's government still counts transactions with citizens, in the future it will count solutions achieved for those citizens. Where today's public workforce focuses on activities, future employees will focus on the outcomes they have achieved. Where today's government is organized in hierarchies, the future's will be much flatter, with employees empowered to make more decisions and use more discretion. "Commoditized" work, like the processing of routine information from citizens, will likely cease to be part of government operations, as it will be automated or outsourced. What will remain will be higher-value personalized work with citizens, which will be performed by better-trained and better-prepared public employees.

The array of digital tools also helps the conscientious employee who, even when she is allowed to exercise discretion by her supervisor, does so under a cloud of worry about risk. Grading risk on the part of others, inherent in the job of many public employees—whether in a troubled family or in a prison, or in issuing a permit—carries risk to the grader as well. Leaving the child in the home or placing the inmate in minimum custody or work release always carries with it professional vulnerability to the person making the decision, thus inadvertently affecting judgment and resources. Data-driven decision making assists the public employee, ensuring higher-quality and more reliable conclusions, along with more protection when one of those decisions goes wrong, as it inevitably will.

Searching for Scofflaws

No story better illustrates the power of data to empower employees than that of former New York City finance commissioner David Frankel. Frankel came to city hall from a Wall Street banking job, bringing with him an unrelenting commitment to data. A tough New Yorker with a compassionate side, Frankel saw tax collection as a profound test of government's commitment to equality for all. Incomplete enforcement, he believes, favors those who abuse the system and tilts the tax burden unfairly toward those who follow the rules. He was determined to use data to make the system fairer.

One way to produce more revenue would have been to simply increase the total number of audits. But Frankel worried that Finance Department auditors employed insufficient precision in the choice of corporate taxpayers to target. Increasing the number of audits, even if he could get more staffers, would also have increased the number of legitimate companies that had to cope with the costly audit process.

Frankel had a better idea: apply digital tools to increase the productivity of his auditors. Using sophisticated data analytics, the commissioner had his department look for anomalies and patterns in the city's vast trove of information about taxpayers. One tactic, for example, flagged businesses that were paying less in taxes compared to others like them. With these analytical tools, the Department of Finance created the Data Intelligence Group to create models that suggested candidates for audit. In their first three years, these models produced assessments and back payments of $292 million, including $27 million from companies that had failed to file tax returns at all. The data analyzed encompasses all business and individual income and excise taxes, plus state and federal tax information, as well as nontax information from other governmental agencies. These modeling efforts include comparison of reported income and expense data across multiple sources. This approach identifies underreported income and turns up the nonfilers. The efforts of the Data Intelligence Group reduced the portion of audit cases that close without any change from 37 percent to 22 percent over three years, a 41 percent increase in productivity. New York City's Finance Department has replaced a shotgun approach to its job with an approach that focuses finite resources on targets most likely to merit scrutiny.

The Frankel story shows us the path to operational excellence: taking advantage of existing data, mining information from other sources, and assigning a well-trained team that asks the right questions and creatively applies algorithms. Thanks to data tools, New York's tax auditors can take pride in the fact that government more fairly funds its work by carrying out more efficient compliance.

Los Angeles County also uses data analytics to uncover fraud. For years, a paper-based check-in system for children in day care made both accountability and auditing difficult for these services. Switching to digital record keeping, which uses "smart" ID cards for tracking children, has been shown to reduce costs for honest providers and give government officials more tools to catch dishonest ones. The Department of Public Social Services uses a series of algorithms to analyze its systemwide data, highlighting outliers in the data that may reflect problems. The system points to child care providers whose records indicate the possibility of fraud, helping investigators to concentrate on the likeliest suspects. This technology allows the agency to take a proactive stance against fraud—a far more effective approach than waiting for tips to come in over its hotline. And, of course, there's a morale boost for employees of the department, who know their work helps get the highly sought-after child care vouchers in the hands of those who truly need them.

Policing with an Arsenal of Data

City governments today expect police to operate inside a system driven by strict rules about everything from when to use a gun to how to fill out a ticket for jaywalking. Within these narrow limits, officers are asked to exercise their judgment in situations where they must make split-second decisions. Yet they have little real-time information about the situations in which they must act. Tomorrow's officers will have all relevant information, constantly updated, about conditions that could affect their work. Digital devices will quickly assemble all relevant information about, say, a suspect stopped for interrogation or a passing license plate. Such data will help officers identify whom they should stop or investigate. That will make them more efficient and effective. Just as with the Department of Finance, information that increases the frequency that an intervention will result in a positive outcome simultaneously reduces government intrusion into the lives of the innocent and therefore assists in overcoming allegations of improper profiling.

Police departments across the country, including in New York City, are embracing the use of data, a trend dating back to the 1990s during William Bratton's first stint as New York City police commissioner. Bratton began his pioneering CompStat system humbly, with coded pins stuck in maps to track crimes by neighborhood. It soon blossomed into an extensively computerized and enormously successful system, credited with curbing citywide crime by 60 percent. In his current tour as commissioner, Bratton is shepherding in the next iteration of data-driven policing in three areas.

First, Bratton set up the new Office of Workforce Engagement that provides full-spectrum issues analytics capability to understand real-time high-priority concerns of crime, safety, and justice among communities and members of the service—well beyond what's reported in traditional crime reports. Even more important than that and consistent with Bratton's approach to help all members of the force work smarter, NYPD will be pushing this capability out to the commanders—ninety-nine of them—so that they can each do three things at the hyperlocal level: fight crime, address community concerns, and mobilize the workforce. This important advancement reflects a critical alignment of mission and resources in that it expands the goals to include community support, not just crime fighting per se; it flattens the organization; and it sparks innovation.

Leading this effort for Bratton is Zachary Tumin, deputy commissioner of strategic initiatives. Tumin, a former colleague at the Harvard Kennedy School who started his career as a special assistant to District Attorney Elizabeth Holtzman in Brooklyn in the 1980s, understands crime and Bratton's goals and brings an exceptional understanding of how to blend new tools into a revised mission. This is a mission that highlights community responsiveness and empowerment. Tumin explains that "new data will usher in the new age of precision policing that is all about context and conversion. No more one size fits all. And we will add to CompStat a citizen, workforce, and community vitality set of measures and metrics—all will be transparent. Now that's data driven!"

Second, NYPD is creating a critical business process management group to test essential processes where data must flow and handoffs abound—value chains like gun cases where so much has to happen right and too often does not. Tumin adds,

> Lives hang in the balance. NYPD crime control lives on patterns—the faster we see them, the better we can interrupt and divert. Data serves as the fuel in our tanks. Without this data, we are blind to patterns until it's too late. You can have the slickest technology, but if data is dropping on the floor, you actually have no real domain awareness. Sometimes even a great pilot needs to look outside the window to see his real situation.

Third, NYPD is more completely joining the open data movement, sharing data in more usable formats with city agencies (for starters, New York City Housing Authority) and incorporating many other data streams to give partners more clarity concerning what's really going on in underreported crime-prone environments.

NYPD has, of course, exceptional tools and resources, but many other police departments are now also seizing data-driven opportunities. In 2011, the Santa Cruz Police Department piloted a suite of crime-fighting analytics software called PredPol (short for "predictive policing"). That year, Santa Cruz saw a 27 percent reduction in burglaries and a 19 percent reduction in property theft by 2012. Los Angeles neighborhoods where PredPol was adopted in 2012 saw a 13 percent reduction in overall crime, while Los Angeles as a whole experienced a slight rise in crime rate. The key to PredPol's powers is in its specificity. The program, created by researchers at UCLA, Santa Clara University, and the University of California Irvine, anticipates where crimes are likely to occur within prediction boxes as small as five hundred feet by five hundred feet.

Analytics will not replace good police work, but augment it. George Mohler, the Santa Clara University professor who developed PredPol, says that analytics platforms are "another tool police can use to elevate all their methodologies, including their own best on-the-ground instincts. The feedback we're getting is that everyone, from police chiefs down to beat cops, is able to put data analytics into play quickly and effectively."

As tight city budgets drive everyone to do more with less, police departments will be able to reinvent themselves through the use of analytics. In departments using PredPol, data not only enables more efficient management of resources and manpower, but also empowers street-level agents to make the best possible decisions.

Controlling Offenders with Data

Parole can be transformed by analytics just as much as daily policing activities can. Five years ago, Philadelphia's Adult Probation and Parole Department (APPD) oversaw fifty thousand people with only 295 probation officers. With a ratio like that, APPD wanted a way to make sure it was spending the most time on the riskiest individuals in the system. If the APPD could accurately categorize recently paroled individuals as low, medium, or high risk for potential to commit violent crime, the agency could save time and money and reduce the likelihood of violent recidivism.

To better estimate the likelihood of each probationer committing a violent offense, the APPD turned to machine learning. Richard Berk, professor of criminology and statistics in the University of California system, partnered with Ellen Kurtz, APPD's director of research, and Geoffrey Barnes, a criminology professor at the University of Pennsylvania, to feed records from 120,000 closed nationwide probation cases containing nearly nine million data points into a machine learning model. Each record includes dozens of variables, including age, gender, prior zip code, number of previous crimes, and type of offense. By employing machine learning, APPD was able to sweep away their preconceived ideas about recidivism, instead giving their software raw data and instructions and letting it "learn" about the most important indicators of committing violent offenses within the next two years.

Surprisingly, Berk's model found that the violence (or lack of violence) of a parolee's original crime was not a strong predictor of committing a violent crime in the future. Other variables emerged as more significant, including the age at first offense. For Philadelphia, in any event, the real value of the model is less in its research results than in its practical management benefits. The model takes a complicated decision (the level of supervision needed for a particular probationer) and intelligently sorts through all the possible predictors to derive a sensible strategy. Now, when any new probationer registers with APPD, the program assigns him or her a risk category based on the predictors identified, and APPD assigns probationers accordingly.

According to Barnes, one of the key reasons for the tool's success has been the APPD's faith in digital approaches. When they found weaknesses in the predictions, staff could have shrugged off the model as geeky interference in their bailiwick. Instead, flaws led to strong efforts to adjust and build a better model with new or different data. Once again, we return to one of this book's key themes: leadership. This commitment to data-based approaches came from the highest level of the APPD, and that support allowed the team to iterate and innovate despite setbacks.

It is too soon to tell whether overall recidivism among probationers has decreased because of this innovation. However, the model has helped the probation staff handle a 28 percent increase in its overall caseload—and with a staff that is 15 percent smaller than it was before the introduction of forecasting.

How close are urban public workers to this vision of digital empowerment we describe? We tell some success stories in this book, but there is no denying that many barriers still stand in the way. The open data movement that provides public access to data needs to be implemented in a comprehensive and easily visualized manner that identifies public employees, not just those outside government, as key consumers. The Philadelphia success illustrates that access to data, led by a sophisticated agency research effort and augmented by talented data scientists, can produce important breakthroughs when fieldworkers accept and use it.

Accountable Discretion

We don't deny that greater discretion for public employees carries with it the risk of poor performance and outright unethical conduct. It was to prevent abuses that the reformers of the late nineteenth century limited employee empowerment in the first place. In a 2013 congressional hearing on ideas for improving government operations, Representative Darrell Issa, the chair of the House Committee on Oversight and Government Reform, zeroed in on just this problem. In response to testimony about the benefits of employee empowerment, Issa immediately asked if such methods might not lead to abuse such as the decision by the General Services Administration (GSA) to conduct expensive training in Las Vegas. Any advocate of digital governance as a way to increase discretion must be prepared to deal with this question.

We believe that the data-driven "retail" approach to governance will bring more successes than the command-and-control approach, but we acknowledge that the change also brings more risk of a mistake or failure. A newly entrepreneurial public sector will need new forms of controls and monitors. Fortunately, the same digital tools that make employee empowerment possible also provide the means to monitor those employees' performance.

As an example, consider a typical child welfare supervisor who goes through the stacks of her files looking for problems after they have occurred. Consider the ways that her ability to ensure quality work could be enhanced by digital tools. Since any input that a caseworker makes in the field is instantly accessible, with a time- and GPS-based location stamp, the supervisor has only to glance at a screen to tell quickly if a caseworker is behind on appointments or has missed one. Later, language analysis software, applied to the digital records of cases, will turn up instances where a caseworker had used identical words to describe multiple children (indicating a possible lack of attention or perhaps the covering up of a missed interview). The same kinds of tools can also ensure real-time supervision of restaurant or building inspectors. In a nutshell, the technology that empowers workers to solve street-level problems can give their supervisors a clear picture of what those workers are doing and how well they are doing it. Workers and supervisors can now communicate when it does the most good: as the problem is being addressed. Longer term, it gives supervisors a quicker and clearer picture of the areas where a worker could benefit from more mentoring or formal training.

In other words, the new tech tools we describe in this book can reconcile street-level creativity with the need for reliability and accountability in public servants. Mobile devices give elected officials vast amounts of data from their workers—for example, where they make decisions, whether the decisions vary by the circumstances or race of the citizen or place in the city, how many infractions or arrests a particular officer has written up under different particular conditions, and on and on. That data stream is both faster and more complete than the current method of supervision—an endless review of written files. With digital governance, a supervisor can ask for daily alerts for cases not closed, matters that have adverse findings or results, or decisions that could be discriminatory, according to data analytics. Similar digital procedures can also improve the monitoring of contractors and their workers, with data being used to identify contractors with high-risk profiles.

Eventually digital improvements in monitoring will spur a sea change in accountability. Where today most governments measure how well civil servants perform particular prescriptive activities, the digital data stream allows public service agencies to measure outcomes instead. In a future data-driven accountability office, the child welfare department management, in conjunction with its research department and data scientist, will constantly search for the providers who furnish the most effective treatments to specific children and families. The data team will relate the efficacy of services to the characteristics of families, which will help match families with the right intervention. It will also determine when the effect of the provider has reached the point of diminishing returns. That will ensure the state does not pay for more sessions then it needs. Such a system would learn from experience, constantly updating its prescriptions as new information comes in and is analyzed. The result is a system that is more effective at delivering its services and less costly to run.

Much as we value employee discretion, we recognize that it cannot be unbridled. The principle of government accountability in a democracy means that public servants must maintain allegiance to a core set of values rooted in fairness and equity and evenhandedness. This is why, as we explained in the introduction, city governments are organized into structures that limit the power of employees. A century ago, this was the only way to ensure accountability. However, the digital revolution in governance has reduced the need to choose between employee empowerment and strict accountability. With instantaneous flows of information across smartphones and other devices, it is possible to empower employees and increase their accountability.

Data-Driven Hiring and Training

Accountability begins with data-driven hiring. Today caseworkers in social service agencies are hired because they meet education requirements and score well on written tests. In the digital world, human resource directors can look at the backgrounds, skills, and training of caseworkers and find the traits common to those who excel at the job. They can then use this information to help in hiring decisions. Of course, hiring well will not suffice. According to Lipsky in *Street-Level Bureaucracy*, we need "to ensure that people employed by the state to teach, judge, evaluate, and counsel have the necessary skills, experience, and training to exercise discretion properly and most effectively."[4] As the technology allows more sophisticated interventions and more worker flexibility, training will become even more important.

Today training is a weak spot for conventional city government. It cannot afford to give employees adequate levels of training, so government relies instead on layers of tight supervision to prevent mistakes. As technology liberates employees from this constraint, it follows that it must also be used to provide much more training than they have been accustomed to. The responsive city's leaders will need to make clear to employees which rules may be bent and which not. A mayor would want not a single doubt in his workforce about the immovable bright lines, such as those dealing with fairness, equity, honesty, and self-dealing. In a data- and technology-driven agency, training will need to inculcate these core principles and then teach employees how to use data and technology to innovate. Fortunately, digital technology can make training more common, more effective, and less costly.

No other city brings the themes of performance management, training, and employee initiative together better than Louisville, Kentucky. Its business-minded mayor, Greg Fischer, ran for office promising to use data to change the way the city operated. One implementation of this pledge is LouieStat, a rigorous performance management system. The system has helped corrections director Mark Bolton push his department to operate at peak performance. For example, LouieStat helped Bolton correct a key underperforming area: the submission of fingerprints to the state. Every month, the state police would send back four hundred to six hundred sets of unreadable prints.

Despite this consistently high error rate, no one ever did anything about it; the reports were simply filed away and forgotten. But then Bolton used the LouieStat model to examine errors by shift, day of the week, and other factors. He discovered common threads: the same officers were taking incorrect prints every month because many shifts had no employees trained in taking prints. Simply providing training to more officers caused the number of rejected prints to drop almost overnight to single digits. The striking success of this use of data to solve a problem has percolated throughout the department, and they have even incorporated the LouieStat model into the department's training academy, which provides training to newly hired recruits as well as skills training and professional development for all officers. Bolton proudly proclaims: "The training and data combination is now going through all layers of the department and other folks are coming up with ideas of identifying problem areas and using data associated with them as opportunities for improvement. It's been a culture-changing event; we've got a long way to go, but we are working very hard at using that model. The approach has been to educate, inform, and motivate people, and to model the way we should act, and by doing that way, it's creating more buy-in."

Open Source Empowerment

One by-product of hierarchical command-and-control systems is they tend to suffocate creative instincts of public employees not just by the inhibitions of prescriptive supervision but also because talented employees with ideas need access both to information and to others in the organization who can authorize change. Digital tools punch through these barriers, empowering workers by facilitating a flow of new ideas through both employee collaboration and procurement.

For example, IdeaHub allows each of the federal Department of Transportation's (DOT) operating administrations to collaborate on ideas that will save money or produce better services. According to the DOT, IdeaHub engages 30 percent of employees, has garnered more than seventy-five hundred ideas, over ninety thousand ratings, and nearly twenty-five thousand comments, and more than one hundred employee-submitted ideas have been adopted.

Hierarchical command-and-control barriers, however, will not fall easily. In 2010 New York City announced with great fanfare the creation of an employee crowdsourcing program. The project involved three hundred employees who collectively developed a range of ideas for improving city government. The idea was that the employees would commit to their ideas and spread them among colleagues, making the project an engine of innovation, not just a suggestion box. The pilot produced a number of sound ideas, among them a centralized research and development unit, a web-based portal for the city to sell items it was disposing of, just-in-time management of inventories, and microtraining sessions for city workers with internal experts. Yet once the pilot ended, the vast majority of public employees never opted into the program. Many expressed anxiety about offending their supervisors by suggesting an idea outside the usual chain of command. One of us (Goldsmith), who had strongly supported the program as deputy mayor for operations, found himself accused by a union of an unfair labor practice. His offense? Proposing to reward individual employees for good ideas.

Today's typical government procurement system suffers the same disease as the human resources systems that are designed to minimize risk and ensure compliance, in the process discouraging new approaches to any problem and favoring existing systems and incumbent providers. Procurement punishes problem solving and aspiring vendors in two ways—the manner it uses to approve providers and the tortuously long and prescriptive method with which it procures.

Few systems in the country are as well intentioned and agonizing in application as the New York City Vendex system used to register and review companies hoping to do business with the city. This process, requiring dozens, if not hundreds, of hours of painstaking time by both the company and the city, can take months to reach a conclusion. Preventing the city from doing business with unscrupulous or criminal companies of course is a laudable goal, but are tedious reports really the best process?

Although the process to register as a vendor remains complex and time-consuming, changes now provide the foundation for using the information in order to identify those who should not be doing business with the city. The Mayor's Office of Contract Services (MOCS) integrated the data into the citywide data warehouse so its information could be used by the Mayor's Office of Data Analytics. But the ability of MOCS to examine other agencies' data as part of the registration effort remains critical but elusive.

Tomorrow's procurement officers will not rely on the same familiar faces. Instead, data mining will be used to create profiles of companies that should be selling products or services to the city—even if those companies themselves don't yet know that they're a good match. And once a vendor is in sight, digital information tools will be used to assemble and analyze data in order to assess how well the vendor organization complies with applicable health, safety, and quality standards. Other algorithms will check the names of those associated with the vendor against all claims by the city or state for back taxes or other delinquencies. Today's monstrously long filings and agonizing certification procedures will become a thing of the past. This newly simplified procurement process will allow the basis of decisions to move from the quality of the vendor's filing to the quality of its solution. Mastery of data and analytics will allow cities to procure the best available solution, not merely the procedurally safest one.

The benefits of abundant data won't be limited to finding and assessing particular vendors. Digital transparency will allow procurement officers to compare experiences and insights with colleagues from other cities and states. Technology procurement will be more about collaboration and relationships than pricing by the unit.

As digital technology helps rationalize procurement processes, it will also drive the desire to rationalize further. The current system of developing specs and seeking bids is simply too slow to serve high-tech needs, says Chris Osgood, codirector of the Boston Office of New Urban Mechanics. "With many of these more experimental tech projects, the specifications you wrote at the beginning of the year can be outdated by the end of the year," he says. "Consumer demands, available technology and interrelated systems are changing so quickly that the projects you work on have to keep pace."

Technology demands greater flexibility than government now has in its choice of partners (but that flexibility, Osgood adds, makes digitally enabled transparency and accountability all the more important). At the moment, he says, incumbent vendors and archaic rules prevent entrepreneurial technology solutions and strategic partnerships. The costs imposed on government to protect against procurement abuse today produce hundreds of times more costs than the abuse itself. Fewer rules combined with the "disinfectant of sunshine," he believes, will produce a better result.

How might a more flexible yet accountable government procurement system work in practice? Some successful early experiments suggest some answers—for example, the federal GSA's Challenge.gov portal. As we described in the Introduction, it's a website where federal agencies pose challenges and offer modest rewards for their solution. That approach creatively sidesteps the many roadblocks the conventional current procurement process poses for public sector innovation. Challenge.gov uses neither a narrow prescriptive procurement nor an expensive government contractor. It doesn't rely on an incumbent vendor. It does not assume that government already has the solution and simply needs a vendor to execute it. Instead of paying first and hoping a solution is delivered, the GSA minimizes its risk and encourages creativity by simply inviting potential solutions from the public.

The approach has the added value of encouraging innovation and entrepreneurship outside government. As we mentioned in the Introduction, one of Challenge.gov's success stories is Nomorobo, an app that eliminates robocalls and telemarketing calls. It was because of his success at Challenge.gov that Nomorobo's inventor, Aaron Foss, was able to found the Telephone Science Corporation, intended to further develop Nomorobo and perhaps other related products. For twenty-five thousand dollars, the Federal Communications Commission's prize for a successful anti-robocall app, which Foss split with a co-winner, the agency gave the public a valuable product and midwifed a new company.

Accountable Discretion by Proxy

Increasingly government delivers its goods by proxy—through contracts with for-profit or nonprofit organizations whose employees usually possess more freedom to innovate and often more data on results. These agents of government, these third-party proxies, often combine better use of data with more discretion on the part of their employees, freed from some of the nonsensical restrictions of bureaucracy. Yet this data also allows the government manager of these third-party contracts to better manage the performance of these partners.

Social Impact Bonds

In the social service area, what are called social impact bonds or pay-for-success contracts allow governments to minimize the upfront costs and risks of initiating new social programs. In these types of contracts, nonprofits and investors bid to run programs to achieve certain results, and the government pays only if those results are achieved. For example, in an ongoing project to reduce recidivism at New York's Rikers Island jail, the contractors have a broad array of tools they can use, unrestrained by the usual features of categorical funding. But their reimbursements and bonuses are based on surpassing baseline targets of reducing recidivism. In this way, government grants the contractor discretion that often exceeds its own: public employees constrained by tight grants, collective bargaining, and civil service rules cannot nimbly respond to critical needs, but the social service contractor measured by results can undertake what works. If the data shows that a particular type of young offender is more susceptible to drug abuse, the contractor can quickly move resources to that purpose.

New York City's Business Improvement Districts

Quasi-government functions, like economic development corporations or nonprofits producing public services, also often benefit by combining less restrictive work rules with metric-driven assessments of their performance.

These kinds of partnerships benefit greatly from digital technology. The enormous success of the Bryant Park Business Improvement District (BID) in Manhattan illustrates one example of a data-driven approach that combines metrics with employee discretion. New York has sixty-eight BIDs, but Bryant Park is one of the best known because it succeeded so well in converting a drug-infested urban area into one of the country's most successful civic spaces.

Dan Biederman, cofounder of the Bryant Park BID and other urban management districts, leaned forward intently as he explained that he measures everything in his quest to maximize the "customer experience." In his office, colorful charts show off items like crime by the hour, maintenance issues, carousel rides by time of day, attendance for every outdoor movie event, and social media posts that are about, or located in, Bryant Park. It is this accurate, timely, voluminous information that allows the BID's managers to focus on results (how clean users find the park) rather than activities (number of trash baskets emptied). BID employees are problem solvers, able to see as clearly as their managers and the public exactly which problems and trends are important. Unsurprisingly, BIDs have proliferated in New York City over the past twenty years. Problem-solving employees armed with data clearly show us the path to a more responsive governance.

The Virtuous Circle of Motivated Workers and Satisfied Constituents

Employee empowerment will help public servants personalize their services and solve problems faster. Combined with data analytics, this retail government approach can address problems even before they occur, producing greater constituent satisfaction and trust in government. Meanwhile, of course, greater discretion will encourage public employees, raising their morale and in turn producing even better service delivery. Thanks to digital tools, a more trustful constituency and a more motivated workforce can reinforce one another in an ongoing virtuous circle of improvement.

According to Sergio Fernandez and Tima Moldogaziev of Indiana University:

> Empowerment practices aimed at granting employees discretion to change work processes and at providing them with opportunities to acquire job-related knowledge and skills are strongly, positively correlated with employee encouragement to innovate. These results confirm a consistent pattern reported in the innovation literature: organizations that grant employees ample opportunities to exercise discretion and to learn and grow tend to be more innovative than others.[5]

Such is our vision of an encouraging future for local government, via empowerment based on digital breakthroughs. We are reminded again of Lolita Jackson, who, on Second Avenue, took on a situation simmering with hostility coming from aggrieved and disrespected neighbors. After the creative solutions that her team fashioned were implemented, an even more energetic Jackson and her local government problem solvers had the profound personal satisfaction of knowing they had saved the jobs—and even the life savings—of small business owners who, but for them, would have closed up their stores and lost everything.

Local government today, driven hither and thither by media exposés, has a paralyzing aversion to risk. That fear produces more bureaucracy at city hall and less trust and satisfaction among constituents. Digital governance breaks down paralysis by helping public servants evaluate risks more clearly. This is why we believe the data revolution represents the most important opportunity in a century to create better government and better cities. It is time to empower our essential public guardians to serve the public good more effectively.

| The Data-Smart City

Set behind a swinging half-door in New York City's century-old Municipal Building, the Mayor's Office of Data Analytics doesn't look like a hotbed of digital revolution. On its pale blue walls, where you might expect digital artworks or framed instances of good press, there is exactly nothing. There are no corner offices (or even assigned desks), just paper-filled government-issue steel cubicles that look as if they predate the first PC, sitting on government-issue gray carpet. At the receptionist's station, next to the gray couch, there's a snow globe and a plastic scene depicting some faraway beach.

Only the whiteboards scattered about, covered in sticky notes and scribbles, hint at what this unprepossessing place has meant to the city of New York and to the cause of digital governance. For several years, two of the cubicles here in room 1012 were home to Michael P. Flowers and his team of young analysts—the crew that broke the city's data out of silos and demonstrated the power of information sharing. And, not incidentally, they became the best city data team in the United States, and one of the best in the world.

Mike Flowers is one of those fast talkers who doesn't seem to be in a rush—it's just that he has a lot to say, his right knee often bouncing up and down as he says it in his East Coast urban accent. He has a boyish face, friendly eyes, and a manner that's both casual and no-nonsense.

Between December 2009 and January 2014, Flowers and his tiny pack of recent college graduates worked painstakingly toward a single goal: showing city agencies how they could be more effective by merging their data with that of other agencies rather than hoarding everything. They worked incrementally, first analyzing stale city data. Then they managed to persuade agencies to pool their real-time data into a collective resource that many agencies can analyze in an automated, routinized way. This data aggregation cost the city just one million dollars in staff costs and five million dollars in other spending. For that shoestring budget (by New York standards), the city got a functioning window for all agencies on a vast amount of data from every other agency. The result, nicknamed DataBridge, greatly improved in-house analytic capacity across several agencies, radically changing the city's way of doing business.

It was a colossal achievement. Flowers had to overcome the natural paranoia and "turfiness" of city agencies, plan and carry out discrete projects that would help make the case for cross-agency sharing, and persuade the people controlling the city's finances that spending money on this new and enormous project was worthwhile. And he had to ensure that the project would outlast his personal presence in city government. He succeeded on all counts.

Yet Flowers insists this story is not about him (and, by the way, he says, he's terrible at math). He doesn't even think it's about technology. What he and his team were doing was managing information the city already had so that it could be "easily used by actors who previously had tremendous difficulty accessing the information, for no legal reason," he says. "This is about leadership, and this is about will." It's a very doable thing, Flowers thinks, and it doesn't have to be expensive. "And you sure don't need a Boston Consulting Group or McKinsey to come in and do a slide deck for you to do it."

Flowers often speaks of his quest for data at city hall as "recon" and a search for "intel"—terms he picked up during almost two years in Baghdad working on the legal team that handled the trial of Saddam Hussein. After that tour, he spent two years delving into the minutiae of financial crimes for the US Senate Permanent Subcommittee on Investigations. It was work as a prosecutor and investigator, jobs where it pays to be hard-boiled, cocky, and creatively fearless, that led him into the world of data.

Flowers comes from a blue-collar background in Philadelphia, where his Uncle Louis drove a beer truck for forty years. Flowers's father died when Flowers was young, so Uncle Louis was a major part of his life. After law school at Temple and a stint as a law clerk in Philadelphia, Flowers made his way to New York County District Attorney Robert Morgenthau's office for a job as an assistant district attorney. Top-flight investigative law firm Williams & Connolly hired him away after four years with the DA's office—a group he describes affectionately as a "cult"—but Flowers was looking for adventure. That was how he found himself in Baghdad in March 2005.

It was the Iraqi insurgency, then raging, that taught Flowers the benefits of data-driven intelligence. As an investigator into the acts of Hussein's confederates, he had a keen interest in keeping his sources alive. Flowers was inspired by the young econometricians employed by the army's Joint Improvised Explosive Device Defeat Organization (JIEDDO) who crunched data on past encounters with IEDs (improvised explosive devices) in order to find the safest possible route through Baghdad on any given day.

His investigative work in Baghdad led Flowers to work on financial fraud for the Senate Permanent Subcommittee on Investigations, where he arrived in 2007. Flowers loved his job as counsel for the committee's work on the financial crisis. For him, it had been the perfect job. "I was this lone actor that was just able to do whatever I wanted," he says. "The perfect work environment." Working closely with Senator Carl Levin's staff, he had sent out a flurry of subpoenas and was working toward the "quintessential analysis of what happened." Flowers had been focused on the weaknesses in the financial regulators' reactions to the crisis as well as the shenanigans of the banks. "I actually do believe philosophically that the government constantly [screws] up," Flowers says. In mid-2009, though, the focus of that committee's work shifted from digging into the causes of the financial collapse to digging into how stimulus funding was being spent. The job Flowers loved no longer existed.

So at the age of forty, his wife four months pregnant, Mike Flowers quit. Or was fired. (It was, he says, probably a bit of both.) From his perspective, all that mattered was that he was now unemployed.

His street sense taught Flowers that the world works tribally (an intuition that working in Iraq abundantly confirmed). When it was time for him to leave the Hill, he got advice from members of two tribes of which he is an honorary member: the "national security infrastructure" world, as Flowers calls it, and the New York County District Attorney's Office. A former colleague of Flowers from the DA's office gave him a lead on a job with John Feinblatt, who in 2009 was the criminal justice coordinator for the City of New York. And Michael Leiter, the head of the National Counterterrorism Center, gave Flowers an actionable theoretical framework for what to do when he got the post.

The job turned out to be handling New York City's response to the 2008 financial meltdown. Flowers was named the director of the financial crimes task force, which in fact was a task force of one. He had no staff, no budget. The theoretical framework was built on Leiter's advice: understand the whole landscape, not just the tech stuff.

Flowers thinks the world of Leiter, who had taken on the unenviable job of fusing intelligence information stemming from the CIA, FBI, and NSA following the intelligence failures discovered by the 9/11 Commission. And Leiter was warning him that when an information-sharing enterprise works among multiple actors, the challenges will be cultural, legal, political, and technological. The technology is easy, Leiter told him, as long as you don't buy products you don't need. There are legal challenges in the New York City context but they aren't as tricky as they are in the national security world. Besides, Flowers was a lawyer; he could find ways around civil statutes. So, Leiter said, focus on culture and politics.

Flowers's first move was to be anointed by the deputy mayor for operations at that time, Ed Skyler. Skyler was deeply interested in Flowers's work in Iraq, and they soon developed a strong personal connection. Flowers needed little encouragement to respond to Skyler's questions about his stint in Iraq. "And so Ed laid hands [for me] over the operation agencies" within the city bureaucracy, Flowers says.

From a political perspective, Skyler's backing of Flowers was essential: Skyler was perceived to speak for Mayor Bloomberg. Without that power behind him, Flowers wouldn't be able to get the city agencies to play ball. But the mayor's implicit imprimatur was just the starting gun, a necessary but insufficient condition for Flowers's new role. Nominally Flowers's initial job was to "do something" about the financial crisis by combining data from several different agencies and analyzing the information; if he found something interesting or potentially incriminating, he would hand it to agencies (e.g., the district attorney) that had enforcement power.

As a cultural matter, Flowers had a lot of work to do as of late 2009. He had months of recon in front of him.

Selling an Idea

Flowers is deeply attuned to the culture of experienced civil servants. He was a good assistant DA, he says, because he understood and respected the cops he worked with. Without a trace of arrogance, he says, "I established relationships with very good police officers who brought me good cases and went the extra mile every time for me."

In the course of his Philadelphia childhood and his adult career, Flowers has developed a firmly held philosophy of government: it is anti–big consulting firm, anti-Ivy, and, at its most general, anti-jerk. He has nothing but disdain for young consultants and political appointees who come in "all crew-cutted up and looking shaved and with a thousand-dollar suit and ask you, 'Oh, so how do you pick up trash?'" Civil servants who have been picking up trash for thirty years don't take well to this kind of treatment. They're naturally suspicious because they see people come and go all the time. So while they wait, Flowers says, "They'll just pander. They'll 'yes' you to death." As he often does, Flowers comes back to the tribal orientation he sees in organizations everywhere from Philadelphia to Baghdad. "These agencies are tribal, and they have clans within the tribes."

Determined not to be the ignored jerk in the fancy suit, Flowers turned for help to Matt Rosen, a friend he'd worked with in the DA's office. Rosen would be the soft-spoken, mild-mannered foil to Flowers's more street-smart personality. In their quest for actionable intel from the financial crisis, the pair soon embarked on a half-year of recon, trying to suss out what the "tribes"—the career civil servants—were up to within the city bureaucracy. As others with new ideas have found in city government, they were aided by the fact that, as Flowers puts it, "nobody had any idea what exactly we were doing." He hadn't been so sure himself at the start, but he was quickly finding his feet.

During this recon period, Flowers knew he had to avoid looking as if he were stomping on any agency's turf. He needed to persuade the DA's office that he wasn't planning to bring cases; he needed to persuade the Police Department that he wasn't even asking for police data; he needed to persuade the Department of Investigation that he wasn't going to encroach on their efforts to root out financial crime. And all of this was true: his mental model was the idea of setting up an intelligence agency that would serve other agencies as clients, feeding information but not seeking to act on it, tailoring its products to clients' needs.

Flowers and Rosen bought a giant whiteboard and started making notes about what the city already knew that might be relevant to financial crime. They pulled together formal organization charts for the civilian agencies whose foot soldiers are out in the streets, getting things done (licensing businesses, inspecting work sites, and so on). Then they created the "real" organization chart for authority over particular datasets. Whatever the formal chain of command in an agency, Flowers says, he had to know that for any particular department "it's actually Jimmy in the IT division who will get me that sample." And Flowers started using his iPod as a thumb drive, "just kind of running around from agency to agency saying, 'Give me a sample of that.'"

Despite the occasional setback, Flowers and Rosen added to their whiteboard every day, and their trove of information grew. By mid-2010, the two men had an idea for a service they could provide to the Manhattan DA's office: better targeting of mortgage fraud cases, based on analyzing data from diverse sources including property transactions and permitting and construction data. Mortgages made up a $1.5 trillion market in New York City each year, and during the period of Flowers's review he believes hundreds of millions of dollars of this flow were fraudulent. Prosecutors would certainly be interested in a way to strengthen enforcement.

It was time to hire someone who knew something about math.

Identifying and Preventing Mortgage Fraud

In Baghdad, Flowers had seen how the analysis of data about insurgents' tactics could save lives. This useful intel emerged from a collaboration among the Army, Navy, Air Force, and civilian contractors—groups that generally protect turf more often than they share information. Flowers eventually received top-secret clearance and got some sense of how data was transformed into intelligence that prevented deaths. But from the beginning, he'd been more impressed by the people generating these data products: "stats" people, all in their mid-twenties, with specific training in computer science and economics.

Flowers didn't want or need official word from the DA's office that it wanted to use a data product coming from the mayor's office. DAs, he says fondly, are a famously cultish group; they're always wary of being big-footed. (As a member of the tribe himself, he should know.) Rather than hard-selling the data product, Flowers realized, all he had to do was show prosecutors that they shouldn't get in the way of its creation. It would help identify mortgage fraud more quickly and accurately. Who could be against that?

To create such a data product, Flowers thought, he needed "a kid that was like that roomful of kids I saw in Baghdad." So he did the obvious thing: he put an ad on Craigslist.

The ad, he recalls, asked "for every skill under the sun that sounded mathy": economics major, some computer science background, skill in Excel, programming languages. Craigslist delivered. It turned up Ben Dean, an impeccably credentialed, whip-smart young man born and raised in Brooklyn's Park Slope neighborhood who had just graduated from Pomona College with a major in mathematical economics. But what sold Flowers on Dean was that he was perfectly aligned with the no-jerk philosophy. In fact, Dean was the friendliest, nicest kid Flowers had ever met. Personality mattered for this hire, perhaps even more than skills, Flowers says, because Dean was "going to have to sit down in front of some street inspector or agency or DA or cop and if he comes across like an arrogant [jerk], we're done."

What sold Dean on Flowers was that Flowers was "extremely confident and cool." And as they worked together, the impression held. Flowers always made Dean feel as if he was doing a great job; he was extremely supportive and sheltered Dean from any tricky politics. "Mike definitely did a good job of just having confidence [in me] and not making me feel too nervous" about how much was riding on his success, Dean says. Flowers also made a practice of bringing Dean with him to every meeting he could. In fact, he'd fight for Dean to be there.

Dean was impressed at how useful Flowers's no-jerk philosophy was for their work. The boss was a great listener to the people in the agencies. "He never assumes he really knows what's there … until he talks to someone who's really an expert in the back room, [the] on-the-ground-dealing-with-the-data kind of guy," Dean says. As a result, he says, information poured in, and "nothing was ever dull" in the "small, mobile, guerrilla unit" Flowers was running.

Dean's first assignment was the mortgage-fraud project. He looked at the data on about 150 mortgage frauds sprinkled across New York's five boroughs with one question in mind: "What did the city know in its property and building records at the time this fraud happened that could tell us that this transaction needs scrutiny?" He was looking at all the data from different agencies in one picture, combining the data about buildings the way the police department combined all its data about a crime.

As Flowers and Rosen had suspected, it was indeed possible to find indicators of fraud in the layered data. Dean's analysis became the basis for a risk filter for mortgages. He and Flowers created forms (with appropriately governmentesque acronyms, like Suspicious Activity Report, or SAR, and later an Unusual Property Activity Report, or UPAR). These could be used by the DA's office to focus prosecutions on likely fraudulent activities. It was a proof-of-concept demonstration project, but it showed clearly that the filter would have helped in the allocation of prosecutorial resources. It was clear, Flowers says, that "the metrics we found looking at city data were very good at predicting whether or not there were shenanigans afoot in a transaction."

But the intel wasn't used. No one was investigated as a result of the filter. A crime needs a victim, and in these cases the victims were banks—and banks don't come forward. For them, the economics of prosecution didn't make sense. From the banks' perspective, even four hundred million dollars in mortgage fraud amounted to a rounding error in an enormous market. Moreover, a prosecution would taint that entire market with the possibility of fraud and make it hard to sell mortgage-backed securities. Without victims willing to prosecute, there could be no case. Actionable insight wasn't acted on.

So, Flowers says, you could label the effort a failure, but he didn't see it that way. He now had proof that there was a real payoff to having a real-time database of everything the city knows about its buildings.

In addition, he had begun to build his team of researchers. They were all "kids with very little experience." He did not want them to come in with assumptions about the way things should be, because he wanted to change the paradigm:

> Bloomberg had one term left, and who knew who they were going to bring in, right? So this was our chance to make a paradigmatic shift this time, right now. It was the perfect opportunity … If I brought valuable product to the table, to wit, information to which [agencies] had previously never had really automated routinized access [to], that allowed them to do things, then that would be a paradigmatic shift rather than a shift that comes from political muscle.

Friendly, unthreatening young city hall employees, just asking sensible questions, would be the agents of this revolution.

A Joint Push from Top City Hall Officials

During summer 2010, two additional New York City efforts focused attention on Flowers's work and its potential. Deputy Mayor for Health and Human Services Linda Gibbs, whose work is highlighted in chapter 7, began her initiative aimed at creating a data exchange and analysis capacity across the many agencies involved in human services. And one of us, Goldsmith, then deputy mayor, had taken over Skyler's job running city operations and the 311 service. Goldsmith had begun advocating for a data analytics center to be based in the mayor's office and was lobbying for funding from the federal Office of Management and Budget (OMB) to jump-start the effort.

As Flowers's work grew, he needed a place to put his hypothetical data-sharing facility, something that would require money for hardware and software, so he had to go to OMB. Flowers has a healthy respect for OMB's ability to say "no" (as a libertarian, he personally hates giant government projects that go nowhere), so he joined with Goldsmith in convincing OMB that his proposal would save the city money by improving its services.

Doing recon on the hardware and software aspects of the proposal, Flowers learned that Feinblatt, the criminal justice coordinator, had already created a system called Datashare. Datashare was primitive—"just a digital version of the old pneumatic tube system," Flowers says—in that it only tracked prisoners: it allowed different actors involved in the criminal justice system to share electronic information about uniquely identified prisoners. The system moved information but did not store it or analyze it. Still, it was a systemic start, a process through which some agencies were already sharing data. It was a rare exception to business as usual, where all of New York City's forty agencies and three hundred thousand plus employees were stolidly in their silos, with no ongoing data cooperation. Flowers asked around and found that he was free to obtain copies of anything sent through Datashare and save that data. Meanwhile, he had learned of a relational database, Citywide Performance Reporting, that was already serving as a warehouse for every 311 call made to the city and as the foundation for much of the operational analytics work being carried out by the team working for Goldsmith. Flowers asked whether that database had the capacity to serve as a reservoir for property-related and Datashare data. He learned that "the whole thing is huge, you got all the space you want."

Now Flowers knew what he needed the OMB's appropriation for. He had an existing data warehouse to which he could hook up every agency in town, have data modeled and put into the database, and then make the database able to respond to Google-style queries for each property in it. He got bids for about five million dollars for aggregating the data and called the system DataBridge. With clear savings to the city already shown and a framework for the data already in place, Flowers was confident. And that was before he, Matt Rosen, and Ben Dean went after the fires.

Preempting the Next Fire with Data

During spring and summer 2011, two illegally converted buildings—buildings in which unscrupulous landlords had allowed gross overoccupation in substandard conditions—were the scenes of devastating fires. Five people, including children, were killed. People wanted to know why the city hadn't been able to prevent the disasters or even done anything about complaints it had received about the two buildings in the fires.

The Department of Buildings (DOB), which has jurisdiction over inspections, has only two hundred inspectors to cover the twenty thousand complaints about illegal conversions that it gets each year through the city's 311 complaint line. Only about 8 percent of these twenty thousand complaints end up being about a serious safety risk. It was a perfect instance of a problem where data analytics could help. Were there unnoticed indicators in the city's information that could help its inspectors find the serious safety issues in the noise of twenty thousand reports? The Fire Department had begun, but not finished, an effort to layer its risk analytics over its inspection protocol.

Goldsmith, Gibbs, and Feinblatt formed a task force to work on the issue; Flowers and his team took up the problem; and Ben Dean cracked the code. On the data side, he found that by marrying building identification data with geocoding software, he was able to combine many datasets from across agencies and map that information on top of the huge number of 311 complaints about conversions. On the human side, he had learned an enormous amount from talking to inspectors who told him what was important to them—what their gut reaction was to particular conditions at buildings. Synthesizing all this information, he found that two of the most powerful predictors of high-risk conversions are whether the building's property taxes have been paid in a timely fashion (information held by the Department of Finance) and whether a bank has foreclosed on the property (information maintained by the Office of Court Administration in the form of mortgage default records).

By October 2011, Flowers's team had its results in place. By prioritizing the complaints that triggered red flags because of the presence of these indicators, DOB could get to the most dangerous buildings faster without hiring more inspectors. The city already had the information: the Legos were there; they just hadn't been snapped together. With routinized, automated access to this data by way of DataBridge, the picture changed. It was a fine, clear victory for data-driven governance—a solution that saved both money and human lives.

Indeed, the data also drove operational changes, making it possible for Goldsmith to set up joint inspection efforts involving both the Fire Department and the Department of Buildings—and sometimes even the Health Department—aimed at fixing dangerous conditions in buildings. Both Goldsmith's operational efforts and what Flowers was doing shared a key characteristic: they were working across traditional silos within New York City government.

It is a disruptive story, and not just for the Department of Buildings (which went on to adopt two new risk-based, outcome-based key performance indicators against which to measure itself) and its inspectors. When agencies share data routinely, Flowers notes, the measures that show how well a department is performing will change its relationship to other parts of government. Government employees have always groused in hindsight ("If that Department of Buildings had gone to that place and rousted them, we wouldn't have had this fire," firefighters or cops might say). Instead, they now can get real-time data on how well the Buildings Department is targeting the highest-risk properties. Complaints based on tribal feelings are harder to justify, but so is poor performance. Tragedies, like the deaths in the building that burned down, can prompt officials to coordinate their efforts. The independent risk assessment tools being developed by the Fire and Buildings Departments allowed both to cooperate not just with development of algorithms but also on their street-level work, where they began approaching the highest-risk buildings as a team.

All of this started with DataBridge. Looking back in late 2013, Flowers said that was exactly how he had planned it: "I had this aggressive strategy of building up analytic capacity on an agency-by-agency basis ... [and now] divisions within the Fire Department are fighting over who gets to work with these [internal analytics] guys." (The earlier Fire Department effort to rethink its prioritization of inspections before those tragic fires hadn't had the access to interagency data that Flowers had or his entrepreneurial approach to breaking down barriers.)

For Flowers, the key to digital transformation was to put the pieces in place and then seek out opportunity. "Opportunity will come up," he says, "and it [unfortunately] came up in the form of the fires." Ben Dean says that although each agency knew more about its own data than anyone else did, "they didn't know how their jobs could be made easier by what else existed out there." Without doing small projects, they would not have understood the value of joining agencies' data together.

Success Goes Viral

The success of the fire inspection project had precisely the effect Flowers wanted. A wide range of city agencies wanted part of his client-service, project-based model of data analytics. Flowers's reaction was to take on all the projects he could. "And that just meant a lot of late nights and weekends for all of us." And that was fine because "the more projects you take on, the more discovery there is … And you just get better."

Having relied on Ben Dean as the sole analyst for two years, Flowers was now able to hire two more young people: Lauren Talbot and Catherine Kwan. Dean was the glue, working effortlessly with everyone; Talbot was the one with the technical chops; Kwan was great at giving clients everything they wanted. And all three felt very motivated to work with Flowers, who rewarded them with constant praise, encouragement, credit sharing (Flowers is not one to claim credit publicly), and almost daily free lunches. For Flowers, team cohesion was of the utmost importance.

Being data analysts, the team of course did not treat each new project as an isolated case. Instead, they leveraged each one for the overall cause of digital governance: each problem gave the team a greater understanding of the city and, Flowers says, "a greater understanding of how we could leverage one project on behalf of another." And the more his "clients"—the agencies—were happy with the results, the more information flowed into DataBridge and stayed there, automatically refreshed. The more real-time information was available, via DataBridge, to the agencies, the more valuable and sustainable the facility became. As Flowers puts it, he was "trying to build a system where it wouldn't matter if I was there or not."

It wasn't always smooth sailing. One law-enforcing agency (which Flowers prefers to leave anonymous) that approached the team had building data that Flowers wanted. He recalls saying,

"Give me your intel, I'll promise I'll give you what the other guys have given me. You'll have a better picture." The reaction surprised him:

> And the guy basically says back to me, I don't want it. And I'm like, you don't want it? I've never heard of a law enforcement officer not wanting intel. You know? And he's like, no, because I'll be forced to act on it.
>
> And the thing is, it sounds horrifying, and I admit freely I too was horrified, as was my staff when I had to look at them with glares and say, shut up. But the thing is, he's right. The guy was right. You know, that's the way the city works. If you hear about something, you're going to get stuck with it, and they're already cutting his budget line.

Now that his influence was rising, Flowers was able to tell the agency that he could help with this problem. He promised: "I'll see what I can do about going to OMB and making sure, if your workload goes up, you get new money." Under pressure from both Goldsmith and Feinblatt on Flowers's behalf, the agency relented and played ball.

Though the fire inspection success story had put DataBridge on the map, it was clear that there were still obstacles. In fact, it took the 911 project to make the Flowers enterprise take flight.

Uncovering Efficiency across Fragmentation

As of early 2011, New York City, after nine years of a painful revamp of the city's 911 emergency response system, finally brought the police and fire departments together in a joint center; yet this had not produced true integration and use of the applicable data even after two billion dollars of investment. Bruce Gaskey then arrived as head of the city's Office of Citywide Emergency Communications Services (OCEC) within the Department of Information Technology and Telecommunications, aimed at integrating previously separate emergency response systems. Gaskey had the thankless job of trying to deal with both the Fire Department and the Police Department—traditionally not thought of as allies—as well as the OCEC and Verizon. None of these actors had married their data to those of any of the others; there was not even a single identifier data field that united the data drawn from all the systems that made up the city's 911 service.

It wasn't just fields full of text that made 911 data hard to quantify and analyze. The nature of the service also played a role. Emergency calls create an information flow that's constantly changing (a call about loud noise turns into a call about a hammer in somebody's skull; five calls in quick succession turn out to be about the same crisis). This makes the meaning of call data difficult to parse. "So, for example, if a PD officer arrived to cover a domestic dispute and then saw someone with a knitting needle in his neck, that's actually two separate transactions, but they were timed as one 911 call. We needed to figure that out," says Flowers. And the work had to be done in a political mine field. If the Police Department or the Fire Department decided they were being criticized unfairly, they could crush the revamp entirely.

Nonetheless, Gaskey wanted to do an end-to-end analysis of 911 calls to figure out who was really doing what that was adding time to the city's responsiveness. When the upgrade was launched, Bloomberg said, "I don't understand why we're spending two billion dollars for 911 and we can't tie the data together." That sent Gaskey to Flowers's team for help.

Gaskey and Flowers bonded immediately. They were from the same Philadelphia neighborhood and had the same salt-of-the-earth dogged brilliance and gallows humor. They're both Irish, so the sample week they picked for all the relevant data inputs included March 17—St. Patrick's Day. The choice wasn't just in homage to the old sod. They wanted to see a day of intense 911 activity surrounded by days with low call volume. Gaskey used his authority to get data from the previous St. Patrick's Day week on thumb drives to Flowers. As Flowers says, "We needed to show that in the end, it would be worth the sledgehammer we would apply to get all of it into the system for use." Meanwhile, the agencies kept assuring Flowers and Gaskey that what they were trying to do could not be done.

That was when the value of Flowers's hiring criteria kicked in. He'd hired Lauren Talbot as a stats person, but it turned out that she was a coder. Talbot had a strong statistics background and knowledge of SAS from her previous job at a consulting firm in San Francisco. She was able to do a lot of technical heavy lifting and significantly streamline the processes Flowers and Dean had originally conceived in Excel. "She comes on her first day and she starts hacking at the terminal," says Flowers. He hadn't even known he needed this skill. He thought, *This is amazing. This is a weapon.*

Talbot started asking questions about the data Gaskey had brought in. She toured the 911 call center to see how it looked, hoping that that would give her some insights into what the various data fields from the different agencies meant and whether they could be connected. And Talbot came up with a way to link these various data sources together.

Talbot noticed that each operator's desk in the call center had a number on it. Then she had an "Aha" moment. The desk numbers, she realized, were the key. She was able to tie an existing "Oper" field tied to a number in each of the thirty thousand daily calls to the tracked phone number from which a given call had come. And she could use assumptions based on the setup—one operator in each seat, each operator handling one call at a time—to screen out noisy data. Flowers loved this: "It was a very interesting mix of qualitative and quantitative [work]. Just true investigative work, plus really solid statistical and data work." Suddenly the Legos snapped together. The team could see every element making up the time between a 911 call and the city's response and could map the statistical outliers.

Flowers and Gaskey took this initial result to Deputy Mayor Cas Holloway, who had succeeded Goldsmith. Holloway is an intense young man who is emphatic and concise. He doesn't suffer fools and has the same kind of "let's get it done now" energy that flows from Mike Flowers. "So then he [Holloway] basically does what Cas does, which is just nuke the place. He called everybody at FD, PD, EMS, etc., [and said], 'You will work with Flowers's team, and I want this done on a weekly basis.'" With Holloway and Flowers joined at the hip, Flowers gained even more credibility with the Fire Department and the Police Department.

Holloway had immediately understood the importance of what he called the Talgorithm. Even more important, he was willing and able to use his power to override resistant agencies and act on his understanding. Having the deputy mayor drive the reform was essential. According to Flowers, "The mayor asked why this hadn't happened before. My answer to him was that this was really a matter of will and capacity."

The 911 project will likely shake up many elements of city government. The city can now use 911 data to manage for better results (Why are internal rules of agencies slowing down responses? How could we better serve the city?). As Holloway puts it, the Talgorithm allowed the city to connect the dots for all segments of a 911 call. "We can now break the data down to show the whole story from picking up the phone to the ambulance arriving, and then measure what we've tied together, which reveals the pain points for calls." The city is not even sure yet how to use this information. But Flowers and Holloway are confident that there is no going back. Now the city just needs to automate and routinize its response to the patterns revealed by its finely grained knowledge of 911 call data.

Flowers is understandably proud of what his team accomplished:

> We now know who the outliers are. We can routinize good practices and eliminate the bad ones. Service providers could go faster by blowing through every red light, or they could squeeze the script and tweak the human management. We can now map these transactions very granularly. This is all about delivery of services. The agency delivering the service can see where, perhaps, labor is being misallocated. You can't run from this data. It is what it is ... I called twenty cities. No one else does this granular transparency, or can. It has a cascading impact. It affects how a city interacts with its personnel.

Analytics Meets the Open Data Movement

In April 2013, Bloomberg signed Executive Order 306, officially establishing the Mayor's Office of Data Analytics. Mike Flowers was named chief analytics officer and chief open platform officer. With that last title, Flowers was named the leader of the city's efforts on open data: making government data available to the people government serves. New York's open data law, he notes, is the most aggressive in the United States. But Flowers is particularly focused on how useful open data can be for internal government operations. When data is routinely released to the public, as the New York City open data law requires, it is also being released to sister agencies. No one has to hunt for the data or know whom to call for permission to access them. That alone eliminates data silos and operational silos.

Flowers is particularly proud that he has worked with city agencies to build up their internal analytic capacity. The Fire Department amplified its use of data, adding data analysts of its own, and the Department of Finance (led by its commissioner, David Frankel, whose success we featured in an earlier chapter) has made great use of DataBridge to better understand tax fraud in New York City. DataBridge now includes statistical analysis tools that permit cross-agency data analysis from over forty city agencies, and all the data is keyed to a common set of geolocational identifiers for New York City's buildings. Eventually, Flowers says, agencies will have to participate in the data flow in order to take advantage of it: to get access to DataBridge, an agency will have to be feeding in its own data.

Most of all, Flowers is proud of how his team got this work done. "We did it honorably," he says, because his team "was driven by doing the right thing … [making city government more efficient and effective]." Getting New York City to use more intelligently what it already knew, enabling the city to tap into its own knowledge so it could improve its services, was the goal. "The data genie is out of the bottle," Flowers says.

Mike Flowers, who had been hired with a vague mandate to "do something" about financial crime, ended up contributing to a paradigm shift in how cities are governed. It's no surprise, then, that his young team members felt an enormous sense of achievement. The mayor embraced his work.

Flowers will say he was building on Bloomberg's vision that people have the right to expect their government to be as well managed as the most modern organizations in the world, and that what he and his team did for citywide analytics was the natural culmination of twelve years of steady and wide-ranging reforms that used technology to create transparent and measurable government performance at a previously unimagined scale.

But Mike Flowers is also a new kind of civil servant, far from the old model of a time-serving bureaucrat doing a single repetitive job. He was there to help agencies solve problems, and he was able to do so intelligently and creatively by using data. He operated with enormous self-generated discretion and ultimately had the benefit of unparalleled support at the highest operational levels of the Bloomberg administration. He started small without trying to take credit, and he got a lot done.

From the beginning of his time in New York City in 2010, Flowers was acting instinctively and having a lot of fun along the way. He made up his own job, and it ended up requiring "a certain measure of intellectual curiosity, love of the city, and a desire not to lose," he says. Flowers had all of these things in spades.

Because of the work of Mike Flowers and his colleagues across city hall, future civil servants will be able to assume the presence of processes that handle much of the commodity work of government—collection of data, service delivery portals, automated licensure processes—and pivot to use these assets to streamline, personalize, and improve the quality of services. Flowers now feels confident that although he has moved on, the DataBridge system will continue to work; that was part of his plan, because "anything that requires constant manual pressure is designed to fail."

Ben Dean expects that in five years, most agencies routinely will be using other agencies' data to inform what they're doing. And he says new government employees, people in his generation, should "come in assuming that they don't know anything" and get their hands dirty understanding how agencies really work on the ground. That's what he did with Michael Flowers. "I think any smart person can come in and, if they're curious, they can find out a lot of things and make a big difference" using data, he says.

At the end of the Bloomberg administration in December 2013, Flowers said that every step he took was aimed at removing any possible cultural or political roadblock to the sharing of information that, analyzed as a whole, would reveal actionable insights that would help the city deliver services better—in effect, doing for New York City what JIEDDO had done for the military in Iraq. The goal was an analytical, data-driven city government where everybody was sharing information in an automated, routinized way. It's not just feasible and desirable, Flowers says.

Despite tradition and tribalism and fear of change, it is eminently doable:

> If I, with no mathematical background to speak of, can take the largest city in the country and get them to rethink how they go about doing some of the most fundamental things in their city government, using kids that I got on Craigslist and lousy computers and stale data, then anybody should be able to do this.

CHAPTER SEVEN

| Rethinking Government

Great quests make for great stories.

There are heroes throughout local government who are battling seemingly impossible obstacles as they push on toward the goals we have laid out in this book: better lives for city residents, more effective and fulfilling roles for city employees, and systemic change in the relationship between city governments and their citizens. Don't let their neckties, pantsuits, and sensible shoes fool you: our heroes cope with fierce enemies, faint-hearted friends, and their own doubts in much the same way as Odysseus struggling to get home, Dorothy journeying through Oz, or Frodo making his way through Mordor.

As much as fortune favors the bold, city bureaucracies favor the timid. Anyone attempting to change a local government must push against legions of lawyers, procurement officers, human resource job classification experts, and others, all intent on avoiding risk—and this list represents only a few of the obstacles to change. We don't suggest this book will overcome these forms of institutional resistance to reform. But we remain confident that local officials can gain strength from understanding how their colleagues in other cities have faced down some of the powerful forces that stand in the way of data-informed governance.

The Story of HHS-Connect

Linda Gibbs grew up in Menands, New York, a small town near Albany. Born into a family that valued public service—her father was the mayor—she found her way to law school at SUNY Buffalo and, in 1988, a role with the New York City Charter Revision Commission established by Mayor Ed Koch. The commission had the ambitious plan to restructure New York City's government, and the energetic Gibbs came in as a staffer. Many of her colleagues would meet again, decades later, in the top echelons of the Bloomberg administration.

Today Linda Gibbs is a veteran of high-level management in New York City, with the thick skin and quiet self-confidence to prove it. Gibbs worked with the Giuliani administration on children's services during an uproar following the 1995 death of six-year-old Elisa Izquierdo, when the city's child welfare system was blamed for failing to protect the little girl, who was beaten to death by her mother. After Michael Bloomberg succeeded Giuliani as mayor, Gibbs became commissioner of the city's Department of Homeless Services. Later, she spent nine years as deputy mayor for health and human services, where a large part of the administration—from the Department of Correction to the mammoth Department of Health and Mental Hygiene, which serves about two million people—reported to her.

Gibbs has a silver bob and bright blue eyes. She listens carefully, nodding and saying "Mm-hmm," encouragingly, then nervously capping and uncapping a pen as other people speak. When she speaks, her hands engage, making large squares with her fingers.

After the Bloomberg administration ended, she followed the ex-mayor to Bloomberg Associates, his new pro bono consultancy—"an urban SWAT team, deployed at the invitation of local governments to solve knotty, long-term challenges, like turning a blighted waterfront into a gleaming public space, or building subway-friendly residential neighborhoods" according to the *New York Times*.[1] From her new perch in the glass-walled interior of the Bloomberg Foundation's townhouse on the Upper East Side, Gibbs is continuing her work with a group of human services practitioners from states and counties around the country. As she puts it, "I want to keep up with what's going on, and take that knowledge and help other jurisdictions who are struggling."

In that capacity, Gibbs thinks a great deal about the challenges that government poses to itself. Her work on HHS-Connect, New

York's digital system for assembling data about individual constituents from across dozens of city human service agencies, is an object lesson. "The project almost died due to the resistance of the lawyers," she says. But it didn't. And Gibbs is full of insights into how to keep such a project alive.

HHS-Connect stemmed from a lunchtime conversation that Gibbs had in 2003, soon after taking over the HHS post, with Martin Horn, the former commissioner of correction and probation. As Gibbs told a Harvard audience in 2009, Horn and Gibbs had some common goals.[2] Both cared about improving the lives of their constituents. Horn wanted to keep prisoners from returning to jail after they left, and Gibbs wanted to reduce homelessness. And their practical responsibilities overlapped: Horn knew that men who had histories of homelessness were more likely to make the round trip to incarceration again.

They decided they should collaborate. In fact, they felt, it would be important for many city agencies to collaborate on homelessness. The first step was to work out a protocol by which employees from different agencies could collaborate effectively on individual cases. So the pair spent eighteen months writing up methods for workers to share their case plans and assessments across agencies.

That turned out to be an enormous mistake. The city had no way of ensuring that a person in one agency database was the same as a person of the same name in another department's files. Similarly, workers in Child Protective Services had no way of finding out if anyone on probation was in the same home as their client. Was the mother of a child in their files getting services from the city's welfare agency? They couldn't find out.

"We realized that it didn't matter if we had a beautiful plan for frontline workers to share case practice," Gibbs says. "You couldn't execute because we were unable, in real time, to let workers know what other agencies were involved with a client. And so that's when we took a step back and started the work on building HHS-Connect."

Their vision for HHS-Connect was basic practical problem solving, aimed at a serious gap in government's capabilities. The system would make available, as a single snapshot, all data about a particular person, drawn from that person's current interactions with multiple agencies. Any authorized city employee could use it. But to avoid any connotation of Big Brother government prying, it would not be a permanent centralized database. Rather, Gibbs says, HHS-Connect would create a "synapse," a connection across the gap in agencies like the connections between branches of brain cells. "Nothing exists unless you say, 'Tell me what's happening with this person, right now,'" she says. "And then when you take your finger off the button, it doesn't exist anymore." You might call it the Snapchat of digital civic technology.

This snapshot function is now beloved by intake workers at the public hospitals of New York City and other city health service agencies. But in order to make it work, data about a particular person locked in the databases of multiple agencies had to be connected somehow. That would not be simple. After all, there are slight variations in records from time to time and place to place, so every time a client is registered with a city health services agency, inaccuracies can creep in. Names get misspelled. Addresses change. To work effectively, HHS-Connect needed algorithms to resolve these kinds of ambiguities as much as possible. That would reduce the risk that two different sets of records from different agencies were actually about different people. The Common Client Index, the nickname for the middleware that made HHS-Connect a reality, collects hundreds of decision rules.

Software wasn't the only issue. To get from point A (no possible awareness of what other agencies might be involved in a client's life) to point B (authorized agency workers seeing everything they were allowed to know about the client's situation) required a major cultural and legal change. The average client was dealing with five different city agencies. In total, nine health and human services–related agencies were involved in the new system. The potential for breaches of confidentiality struck the agencies as high, especially after their lawyers had thoroughly frightened them about the issue. They were not inclined to liberate their information.

The agency that goes into information lockdown is a common problem for advocates of digital data sharing. Gibbs's favorite story about the problem comes from her time as homeless-services commissioner. A homeless-services aftercare worker had gone to check on some clients who had left a homeless shelter for permanent housing (standard policy, because people who have recently moved out of a shelter are at the highest risk of homelessness). The mother in the home was having a tough time with drugs. In fact, her substance abuse worker (from another city agency) was in the home at the moment the homeless services worker arrived. The homelessness worker wanted to share notes and business cards with the drug abuse prevention worker. Forget it, she was told. From the substance abuse worker's perspective, she and her client had been "discovered," and any information sharing violated her client's right to confidentiality. Instead of cooperating with her colleague from the other agency, she ran out the door.

Why would one public servant run from another when they're in the same house serving the same client? From Gibbs's perspective, the problem stemmed from the way agency lawyers interpret a complicated maze of laws. "There's a lot of overapplication and overinterpretation of the law," she says. So lawyers prefer lockdown, in part because it saves precious time, Gibbs says. They say "absolutely no, because who has time to figure out what information we can share and what we can't share?" As a result, perfectly appropriate information sharing among professionals wasn't happening.

Gibbs realized that she would have to outlawyer the lawyers and hired an attorney named Barb Cohen to lead the effort. Cohen methodically researched the law applicable to the most important sources of data to which an authorized city worker might want access to help clients in need. At the top of the list was Human Resources Administration data: records about cash assistance, food stamps, Medicaid status, and Medicaid claims, as well as billions of scanned images of leases, pay stubs, and birth certificates. Other important "source" data would need to come from Child Welfare, Probation, the criminal justice system, and the Housing Authority.

Cohen's careful work corrected some false impressions. In some areas, agencies had their obligations exactly backward. Rather than requiring them to withhold information, the law actually required them to share it. In other areas, agencies were allowed to share under the right circumstances. Criminal justice information was open to the public, so it could easily be included.

Finally, some data, like HIV status and mental illness diagnoses, couldn't be shared at all.

Cohen's detached and lucid analysis persuaded other agency lawyers that she understood and respected the laws that governed their departments. It was important, Gibbs says, that they see that Cohen was as careful as they were about protecting the city from legal risk. Lawyers who say no can terrify department heads. As Gibbs puts it: "The lawyer says to the commissioner, 'You're going to get sued. And do you know you're personally liable? And do you know the city cannot indemnify you for this?'" The commissioner then has to weigh policy progress against his confidence in his attorney and his fear of sanction. "It takes a pretty strong commissioner to balance all of this," Gibbs says. This was why Cohen needed the attorneys on her side. It was a delicate business, Gibbs says, to "make the lawyer feel appreciated and at the same time to make him go away." Persuading lawyers proved to be an ongoing challenge. As the years went by, new lawyers would come to the agencies, and persuasion would have to start all over again.

All of this careful legal work informed the design of the HHS-Connect system, and that comforted the agency lawyers. No depository would be kept. The system would make possible access to just one client's situation at a time. And only the right set of people would have access to that glimpse. Gibbs and her team call this access portal Worker Connect. "The way we built [Worker Connect] is that there is essentially a series of security trap doors. The door will only open to give their workers access if there is a legal basis for their access."

Steadily, Gibbs and her team put in place a series of "use cases" that linked each carefully defined category of worker to the also carefully defined information to which that category can have access. It took about two and a half years. Workers log in to their particular job's use case for HHS-Connect and have access only to information deemed relevant to their work. In Gibbs's view, the opportunities for abuse are limited. All access to data is tracked; if there is a problem, the technology will reveal exactly who did what.

Lawyers were not the only constituency that needed careful handling by the HHS-Connect visionaries. The heads of the affected agencies needed to be kept "in the boat" too. Their potential for skittishness was cultural—Gibbs calls it the

"I'm going to keep all my toys" attitude of commissioners when they feel their sovereignty over IT functions or information is being threatened. So her solution was cultural too. She created an executive steering committee for HHS-Connect. No staffers could be sent to its meetings. Only commissioners (department heads in New York City government) could belong. Gibbs chaired the proceedings, and the entire group, acting as a sort of board of directors, had to approve every step in the process of developing HHS-Connect. Gibbs says this worked; the commissioners "took their role very seriously," and the steering committee embodied the buy-in of all the agencies.

One selling point was that the idea for HHS-Connect had come from a shared city employee interest in doing the right thing for clients. Everyone at the steering committee table could see that when someone is being admitted to a homeless shelter, carrying kids and bags, it's painful to be asked for birth certificates and leases that have been provided to the city government many times before. "They're going through trauma," Gibbs says, her voice rising. "And we're being bureaucrats." The system also had practical payoffs for all the departments, she notes: "Our clients will do better and therefore be less likely to become homeless again or to recidivate."

It also helped that HHS-Connect was built in what Gibbs calls "the old-fashioned way"—with careful attention to the peculiarities of bureaucratic life. The man she tapped to lead the overall project, Kamal Bherwani, was both brash and experienced in government; he muscled his way through to get it done, hired a big firm, and paid them at a significant rate. This worked, according to Gibbs. But when Bherwani's successor, an outsider with vast private sector IT knowledge, tried to bring his expertise into government, "the bureaucratic process of government totally smashed him." He could not figure out how to convince officials to execute his plans and left. After that, Gibbs says, she went back to the old-fashioned way of doing things. She's philosophical about this. "In order to be successful, we've had to find the path of least resistance with HHS-Connect. We had to overcome all of these cultural barriers and make compromises."

Today HHS-Connect is an accepted part of government, accessed sixty thousand times a week. And it even has an interface for the public: a website, ACCESS NYC, that gives citizens a single place to check their eligibility for a host of city programs. Meanwhile, Worker Connect improves collection of data and makes it possible, once data is in, for all of the right workers in the right agencies to see the data. For example, clearance workers in the city's child welfare system—now the largest group using the system—can triage the fifty-nine thousand protective investigation requests they get each year by pulling reports drawn from HHS-Connect. In the city's public hospitals, HHS-Connect is used to help people enroll for public insurance even if the client hasn't stuck around to fill out all the paperwork.

Constituents who walk into a New York homeless shelter now do not have to provide the same information that they have already given to the Administration for Children's Services. Thanks to HHS-Connect, shelter workers can "prepopulate" much of the application. Even better, clients began requesting copies of their own records from the workers accessing HHS-Connect. "The clients then started saying, 'Can you get me a copy of that birth certificate? You have my Social Security card? Can I get a printout of that?'" This was great for these individuals, Gibbs points out, her voice climbing up a notch in delight.

The agency that has most clearly benefited from HHS-Connect is the Health and Hospitals Corporation. Its greater ability to get emergency room clients connected to Medicaid has improved its revenue stream. And for an agency with a seven-billion-dollar annual budget that routinely runs one billion dollars in the red, that is great news, Gibbs notes. "They're cutting costs like crazy. They're struggling to meet their mission. So anything that can help to improve revenues is good." Meanwhile, in the realm of child services, the benefits are more personal. HHS-Connect can help locate absent fathers—or interested aunts and uncles—where a child might otherwise be headed to foster care because of a mother's problems.

Other benefits of the system may not be as easy to quantify, Gibbs notes, but they're unquestionably important. For example, Gibbs says, HHS-Connect can heighten workers' sensitivity to the complexity of a client's life. A worker who sees that quick information snapshot instantly realizes how many other agencies are involved in a client's case. That can motivate the worker to help simplify things for the client—to help that person get a birth certificate and a social security number and do the follow-up by pressing a few more buttons on the keyboard instead of forcing clients to go down the block to another office.

For all its success, though, Gibbs considers HHS-Connect to be a primitive tool. "We've built a dinosaur of a system," she says. One limitation is that workers in the field don't yet have access to HHS-Connect, because it doesn't work on mobile devices. Moreover, she notes, there are still walls in the city's data about each individual client. Then too, the protections that won over the lawyers have limited the tool's usefulness for policymaking. Since the "synapse" disappears after it is called up, there is no trove of data from which patterns and outliers can be found. And HHS-Connect isn't helping workers from different agencies collaborate on case plans, shared notes, or the timing of appointments. It's not there yet.

"In a sense," Gibbs says, "what we did with HHS-Connect was to pick the low-hanging fruit. We didn't try to solve all the problems." Yes, she allows, the system represents "incredible progress." Still, she adds, HHS-Connect is "like the equivalent of the old mobile phones—the size of a boom box and with a huge antenna. But someday it's going to be like this," she says, picking up her smartphone.

The next generation of the conversation about human services will have to include review and revision of the standards in order to convince the Department of Education to share its data. "It bothers me that we have a set of laws that actually get in the way of helping workers to help families because they're not allowed access to the information," Gibbs says. In this area, the trouble may not be, as it was elsewhere, that the laws are interpreted narrowly or misunderstood. Part of this problem may be the laws themselves.

Gibbs's vision, one she's now implementing through Bloomberg Associates, is that workers will have access to the information they need, wherever they are, in real time, so that they can have a broad contextual view of what's going on in a client's life. She aspires to see fieldworkers able to collaborate in real time. She would like to see clients able to go to the system themselves, print their own records, and see their appointments. The future Gibbs envisions is today taking shape in Indiana, a story we tell in chapter 8, with new tools, no "synapse" limits, and the ability to see patterns as well as cases—sharing and analytics. Yet even advanced technology has not made fighting lawyers or agency turfness any easier.

Civil Service Obstacles to Empowering Employees

Rigid job descriptions complement rigid lawyers. It's not surprising, then, that life-improving breakthroughs often come from city employees who have the latitude to do what they feel they need to without the limits of narrow classifications or suffocating oversight. Indeed, one of the merits of digital governance is that it opens up the range of discretion and personalization for city workers, as we described in chapter 5. For example, Mike Flowers, whom we profiled in chapter 6, had plenty of discretion. In fact, he says, his formal title hardly mattered as he set up his "skunkworks."

Yet cities have trouble "broadbanding" civil service roles, thus limiting the opportunity for employees to move from performing activities to solving problems. Of New York City's more than 300,000 employees, for example, 230,000 fall under the jurisdiction of New York State's Civil Service Law. This statute, put in place 120 years ago, is the basis for a civil service system that dictates in exquisite detail exactly what work these employees are allowed to undertake. With more than a thousand civil service job classifications in New York City, narrow roles—like "temporary full-time permanent intermittent police officer"—are common. It's an outdated system that raises the city's costs while hemming in its employees.

Of course, the civil service system and its commitment to merit are necessary to city government. Indeed, the creation of New York State's civil service system launched state assemblyman Theodore Roosevelt's career in 1883. The public was quick to grasp the value of the young legislator's attack on a crony-laden system. But the principles that underpin the system have become lost in a florid growth of complex and restrictive rules that are extraordinarily difficult to navigate. For instance, the city is obligated to rank candidates for its 185,000 competitive-class jobs based on exam results alone. Professionalism, maturity, and job experience can't be taken into account. This means city agencies have very little leeway when picking candidates for a position.

"Some of the steps in the civil system just don't work anymore. The system has been around a long time. It's stodgy," Martha K. Hirst, chairwoman of a ten-member Workforce Reform Task Force appointed by New York's Mayor Bloomberg, told the *New York Times*.[3] The task force was recommending substantial reforms of the system. "We wanted to find ways to get things moving and make it work better," Hirst said.

The task force did indeed do some good. After its report was released in 2011, the city adopted the recommendations that fell under its jurisdiction. City hall consolidated forty job titles and redefined a quarter of competitive job titles so that hiring for them could be based on job seekers' education and experience. But a combination of municipal union unhappiness and unease in the state government blocked the rest of the reforms.

The heroes do not win every battle. Yet as we have described in other chapters, there are enough success stories to motivate dedicated public servants to continue to fight for digital governance and the empowerment of workers that it allows. And we think reform activists need to do a better job of convincing some municipal union leaders of the benefits stemming from empowering employees. In New York City, union leadership felt insufficiently involved in the development of the 2011 reform report and was accordingly suspicious about the intent behind it. The very system in need of changing, one that functions in a predictable but mechanical fashion, builds in resistance to change and creates substantial uncertainty in the face of reform.

Employee Discretion and Creativity

When the forces of good management and labor leadership and technology come together with more workforce discretion, amazing things can happen. For example, in Boston, the adoption of the City Worker mobile app (discussed in chapter 1) gave workers the autonomy to figure out on their own when and how to respond to service issues that had been called into the Mayor's 24-Hour Hotline. Justin Holmes, interim CIO for the City of Boston, notes that this has led to some entrepreneurial behavior on the part of service workers.

Boston's recycling program hands out large bumper stickers to constituents who ask for them, so they can label any trash can as a recycling container. One day, the Mayor's Hotline got a call from a man living in one of Boston's far-flung southern neighborhoods asking for one of these stickers. "And eighteen minutes later a public works employee showed up at his door and slipped one of these [stickers] under his door," Holmes said.

The caller went to the door in amazement. "What are you doing here?" he asked. Holmes reports that the worker said, "You called asking for a sticker. I just wanted to deliver it." The caller said, "I appreciate that. But how, even if you ran every traffic light from city hall, could you possibly have gotten here in such a short time?" The public works employee showed the constituent his iPhone and the City Worker app. "I happened to be around the corner when your call came in, and I had some stickers on the truck, so I thought I'd drop by."

This kind of story is rarer than it should be because of the narrowness of jobs conceived under the old civil service approach and in part because technology to liberate public employees has not yet been deployed widely. Technology can assist, as Linda Gibbs said, by helping to unleash worker creativity and ensuring that discretion is being appropriately deployed—within parameters that serve the original principles that gave rise to the whole idea of meritorious civil servant service in the first place.

Procurement as the Barrier to Innovation

We do not want to leave anyone with the impression that job descriptions and employment rules constitute the only barriers to the technological liberation of public employees. As we have mentioned elsewhere, the procurement process presents another formidable barrier to digital governance today. Any city hall employee involved in technology will simply shake his or her head (or shudder) when the subject comes up.

Although governments around the world spend billions of dollars a year buying software, hardware, and consulting services, existing rules make it extraordinarily difficult to operate with any agility or flexibility. There is a profound mismatch between current procurement rules and the best ways to develop and deploy technology in cities. For one thing, current processes require governments to be extraordinarily specific in advance about what they want to purchase. In a world in which city employees probably do not know what the best solution will turn out to be, officials must commit in advance to a particular approach. Then, too, current procurement policies favor expensive, large contracts. That makes life harder for city governments interested in purchasing innovative solutions that blend multiple providers and open source technology; it makes life easier for governments that seek single-firm, proprietary, expensive software.

As an example, take Massachusetts Law Chapter 30(B), which dictates the procurement processes the city of Boston must follow. For any product or service costing over twenty-five thousand dollars, the city has to follow highly specified "call for bid" or "request for proposal" procedures. (There are weird exceptions to these rules: governments don't have to competitively bid school photographers in Massachusetts.) In general, these highly detailed requirements cannot be met unless the city already knows all of the details that will go into the solution to its problem. By definition, then, they block almost any sort of open-ended experiment. A bid that lacks specificity might easily result in a protest or lawsuit.

The federal government's 2013 healthcare.gov debacle provides a fine example of how government procurement procedures actively hamper digital innovation. Although many failures caused that embarrassing initial rollout, during which only a half-million of the twenty million visitors to the site were able to complete applications for insurance, one stands out: those in charge of the process focused more on the complex rules embedded in procurement compliance than program solutions. Civil servants trained in policy, who focus on the actual problem the technology should solve, did not have the right seats at the table. And so the hard questions they would have asked were never heard.

The trouble is that the comply-with-detailed-rules approach to contracts fails to take into account the speed with which technologies change. When New York City first sought to create the data analytics center we discussed in chapter 6, for example, standard-issue procurement procedures were predicted to take two years to run their course. That was the entire remainder of

Mayor Bloomberg's term. The impromptu work of Mike Flowers through his self-described "skunkworks" helped to sidestep some of the problem by avoiding a process that would have halted citywide analytics changes. Procurement processes that take years are not flexible enough to incorporate new developments. (Today, for example, many functions that used to be run inside municipal governments can now be provided as modular services sold by cloud providers. Procurement processes have yet to fully tap the power of this transformation.)

All of these rules and specifications mean that it takes a very long time for cities to move through these processes. The same applies to vendors or partners: many companies cannot afford the time required to try to get a typical city contract. Smaller vendors, which might be able to provide lower-priced, competitive products, especially are dissuaded from getting in the game. So the winners in the procurement contest often end up being large, incumbent companies.

What can digital governance advocates do to clear away this massive obstacle to reform? Instead of even more attention to regulatory process, perhaps the answer lies in heightened transparency about selection, or results, or impact—all made possible by digital technology. Breaking down large projects into modules, with pricing made clear, would make it far easier for other cities to compare their spending patterns with their peer's. An added bonus is that providing incentives to share the completed requests-for-proposals and the technology procured through such systems with other officials interested in similar innovations would help more cities try their hand at more creative solutions.

The City of Philadelphia's Office of New Urban Mechanics is tackling these kinds of procurement problems head-on. The office wants the city to be able to work with more small bidders, get access to a larger pool of competitive bidders, and generate bidding pools that include the talent of Philadelphia entrepreneurs and tech companies.

So in October 2013, Story Bellows, cochair of that office, announced a program called FastFWD to spur the creation of solutions and then award city contracts to projects developed during the program. Philadelphia selected ten entrepreneurs with innovative ideas about how to address public safety needs to enter an accelerator program. Philadelphia is also planning procurement by way of GitHub, a hosting site for open source software development. Already, says Bellows, Philadelphia is seeing higher-quality responses from its pilot solicitation on that site than it has seen from traditional processes. The city, focused on transparency as well, has launched a simple website to make new tech procurement opportunities visible.

As with the obstacles to hiring and promotion presented by the existing civil service system, the current procurement system was created for good reasons. And as with civil service rules, we argue that new tools lead to reforms that will allow the original goals of the reformers to be more completely fulfilled. We can have more creativity, flexibility, and performance-based contracting and more accountability and transparency at the same time. The point of current rules is to root out waste, fraud, and abuse while getting the best possible value for public money and minimizing the risk that the officials involved in any given procurement will act in their own interests. But over time these noble principles have been covered by a riotous growth of process—often in detailed statutory form, like Massachusetts Chapter 30(B)—that sometimes appears to exist solely for its own sake, not the public's.

Meanwhile, digital technology has advanced. Today the overall purpose of procurement rules—strict oversight and transparency—would probably be better served by using technology. Software code can do some of the work that the legal code used to. A networked, graphical visualization, fed by data and easily accessed by any citizen, would make it possible to see the picture of procurement for a given city in new ways. And big data analytics could target anomalies in contracts or performance in real time, a more efficient approach than using a ham-handed contracting procedure to try to foresee and forestall all waste and malfeasance in advance. Imagine a picture of the outcomes generated by any one procurement measured against all other similar procurements over any period of time; imagine being able to state a problem and then work cooperatively with companies to figure out a joint solution that could scale across multiple cities, with payment to be allocated based on the value-added performance.

Another way to inject vitality into rigid processes is to change the incentives cities offer their vendors. Rather than rewarding bigness and familiarity, procurement rules can encourage more useful traits in vendors. In Stockholm's city government, for example, one guideline for the selection of vendors and techniques is that the procurement stimulates local innovation. In other words, Vice Mayor Ulla Hamilton says, every city department is required to consider how it is stimulating creativity in Stockholm when it puts work out for bid. Department heads know that part of their budgetary reporting will be based on the extent to which their procurements are innovative. Stockholm's internal budgeting system generates a monthly green, yellow, or red dot for each department based on this innovation metric. "And if there is a red dot, the vice mayor will call the department every week to see how they're doing," Hamilton says.

Similarly, cities could go further by creating their local versions of Challenge.gov: they could put technical problems on a site and invite solutions online. This sort of "eBay for procurement" would lower the barriers to collaboration between outside parties and city officials, allowing them to easily work jointly on a project.

Current state procurement laws in the United States slow or prohibit most of these new approaches. Therefore, it's not enough to innovate at the edges of the system and win over its lawyers. Legal reform—actually rewriting state statutes—is required. Just as with employee empowerment, so too with procurement can we have both more discretion and more accountability. Purchasing regimes need to allow more attention to solution and less to cheapness, more to trusted partners with good records and less to elaborate scoring systems that often score the application, not the service or product. Best value, not best price, can be achieved in an accountable, transparent reformed system.

This is not a utopian fantasy. Today, Code for America is working on municipal procurement reform, focusing initially on Portland, Oregon; Kansas City, Missouri; and Philadelphia. All of these cities see great potential payoffs in being able to incorporate smaller, high-value technology providers into enterprise solutions. Dugan Petty, a former Oregon state chief information officer and procurement director, put it this way to *Governing* magazine: "The traditional government RFP process—with its long timelines, complex rules and tight guidelines around liability—tends to scare off some of the IT industry's most innovative companies."[4]

The bottom line is that cities should be able to preserve the public trust and foster accountability by increasing transparency in exchange for reducing the transactional burdens of the current process. That way, cities will increase the pool of bidders, driving down public costs. Even more so, it also allows existing bidders, large or small, to innovate and suggest better processes. Almost every vendor to government we interviewed had a better way to accomplish the task bid by government but had no accepted or welcomed process to present it.

Public value happens to be the point of having procurement laws in the first place. More open results-driven processes will allow large contractors to incorporate more local talent into their approaches. Clay Johnson, former lead programmer for Howard Dean's 2004 presidential campaign, frames the big picture: "Fixing procurement is about local economic development: 21st century procurement processes create jobs. The first city to implement [these] changes ... is in for a massive boom. It'll be able to work with local designers, developers and other innovators within its own community."[5]

And so our heroes sail on, despite skeptics, despite information-hoarding bureaucracies, despite lawyers and their terrifying scenarios of doom, and despite laws designed in a different century for a different century. The reformers' example shows what we know to be the case: they, and the responsive digital governance that can do so much for cities and their people, will prevail.

CHAPTER EIGHT

| Toward Responsive Cities

The people you have met in these pages have convinced us (and, we hope, convinced you) that the digital revolution is American urban government's most promising chance for change in more than a century.

We see three shining opportunities for city leaders willing to embrace the power of digital information. First, they can *empower* government employees to use their discretion and common sense, working toward better lives for citizens rather than simply pushing toward increased, narrowly defined activity. Second, these leaders can *engage* with citizens in the important provision of services, thus thickening the bonds of democracy and the vibrancy of civic life. Third, these digital solutions will *enable* citizens to work with local government on shared solutions to the grand challenges that confront all Americans. Predictive analytics that take advantage of massive amounts of new information will produce cost-effective solutions to chronic problems. Thankfully, we found leaders throughout the country eager to seize these opportunities. At every level of federal, state, and local government, they are replacing rigid hierarchies with fluid, responsive digital systems.

Mayors are leading this great change. Among them, Mayor Michael Bloomberg pushed hard from the top in New York City to make his agencies cooperate in creating a metrics-driven city; Mayor Rahm Emanuel put technical smarts at the heart of his policymaking and made Chicago a place where best practices were born; Mayor Tom Menino put technology at the service of greater constituent engagement in Boston. Importantly, despite significant policy differences with their predecessors, the mayors who have taken office in Boston and New York have not only continued these data breakthroughs but have also built on them. Mayor Marty Walsh in Boston plans major advances in the city's use of dashboards and predictive analytics. And in New York City, Mayor Bill de Blasio has moved strategic tech policy leadership inside city hall. De Blasio also plans to expand his administration's use of data in a range of areas from policing to reducing traffic fatalities.

We will be continuing to follow these developments as they occur and chronicling them on our Data-Smart City Solutions website. We look forward to finding data-driven breakthroughs wherever they may happen. There are many leaders in this field, both within and outside city hall. Remember Daniel O'Neil, of the Smart Chicago Collaborative, running community user testing groups to see whether tech initiatives launched by city hall will work for actual citizens; Kathy Pettit, of the Urban Institute, building the capacity of neighborhood nonprofits to use data to help govern their own communities; and Chris Osgood and Nigel Jacob, of Boston's New Urban Mechanics office, catalyzing the development of the first mobile app for 311.

All of these civic innovators had two things in common: commitment to their goals and freedom to act. The usual terrors of urban politics did not frighten them. Bill Oates's colleagues in Boston said he had a "particular fearlessness." Brett Goldstein, of Chicago, seemed to almost pride himself on his willingness to be fired in exchange for his freedom to do what was right. "Nothing was ever dull" while Mike Flowers of New York City was around, according to his staff. And Linda Gibbs, also of New York City, infused with the passion of her mission, did not give up when fighting against bureaucratic entanglements on behalf of homeless constituents.

These leaders, from the private sector, the ranks of government, and the nonprofit world, are convinced that data makes great things possible. They're also convinced that they themselves can achieve those great things. Part of their success as leaders comes from their ability to impart to others a clear vision of the role of technology in modern life: they all see that the world outside the walls of city hall is changing quickly. Our champions have overcome the frustrating fact that in the slick modern world of always-on, graphics-rich, personalized communication tools, local government is often stuck issuing formal, instantly out-of-date paper memoranda.

These leaders have a knack for getting others to share their vision of the future. That has helped them get things done. Refusing to be hemmed in by their job descriptions, each has been successful in defining his or her own role. They know, because they understand the flow of digital technology, that no career is carved in stone and everyone can help.

Today's confident civic technology leaders know that we are just at the beginning of a transformative time. They recognize that even their proudest achievements are just stepping-stones. ("We built a dinosaur of a system," Gibbs says.) Flowers registered his surprise that people were so impressed with the fire prediction inspection algorithm. "It was clearly going to work because you're going from random to some measure of rationality," he says flatly.

Leaders in this movement exist throughout government and city life, asserting their influence within bureaucracies and community organizations alike. They are kindred spirits, though many of them work in unfortunate isolation. There's the guy in the basement who understands the databases his agency controls and knows how that information might be made useful in a fresh context, but he has no levers to pull that would give him the ability to collaborate across his agency's walls. There's the civil servant who knows exactly how to fix a broken service process but is slotted into a job that doesn't have responsibility for fixing it. There's the community leader who has organized a neighborhood watch but has no straightforward connection to the authorities with resources to fix a broken streetlight. There's the young coder who wrote a piece of software for fun and civic pride—work, she's convinced, that could alter the way citizens understand their local health services. But she can't possibly meet the legal requirements of her city's procurement process. There's the local government official who has a hunch about how to more justly and effectively allocate his city's resources, but has no access to the data that could confirm his intuition.

We wrote this book because we want to celebrate the ideal of future digital governance and hasten its arrival. We hope others will be as inspired as we were by the stories of the people we met who have arduously strained to change the way their cities work. We are glad to see leaders and data activists continuing to pursue even greater successes; these successes build on each other when one innovator sees the results of another and knows he or she is not alone.

The past constantly threatens our civic future through outworn lines of authority, nonsensical rules that have ceased to have any positive effect, and reliance on outmoded ways of working. Yet there are scores of heroes working daily with courage, patience, and kindness in many contexts around the country who wish things worked better and think responsive technology can help. We want to give them hope and encourage them to meet one another.

As Mike Flowers puts it, "The data genie is out of the bottle." Now it is up to all of us not to protect existing governance systems that no longer fit the modern world. Those systems were often built to house paper; to stamp it, file it, copy it, sometimes lose it, sometimes find it, but above all to control it and send it up a chain of command. Now the information that used to be embodied in those stacks of paper has been loosed from its bonds. Disembodied, it's a little frightening; it is unnerving to contemplate the floods of repurposable data that are generated every day by cities. And so, unfortunately, even some of the best civil servants and civic groups unwisely conspire to hang on to what they understand because that is the way things have always been and because to change existing systems would be destabilizing. The people we profile in this book have learned better.

As an integrated whole, the stories we have told in these chapters provide a blueprint for dramatic changes in government. In the past, even those officials who were implementing technology change at the local level undervalued the contributions that technology could make in constituents' lives. Institutional change, accordingly, was incremental. Today people like Mike Flowers and Brett Goldstein are using data and solving problems nominated by city agencies. These data-driven solutions are persuasive and energizing for other government employees, who can suddenly see the benefits of sharing what they know in digital form. And the energetic team in Boston was able to take the vision of Mayor Menino, utterly focused on citizen engagement, and drive it forward using technology. In Chicago, a strong leader, Mayor Emanuel, provided the institutional backing for a systemic approach to responsive city government, unlocking the data resources of the city so that they could be redeployed in the service of all of its constituents. In all of these cities, there are small groups outside government working together to solve problems by using technology that allows them to be heard as coherent, persistent voices in collaborative settings.

We think the combination of these stories is truly powerful. Together they show that effective high-quality responsive governance that engages citizens and thickens the bonds of democracy is possible. We can now use the tools of the future to go back to the principles and methods of basic democratic engagement. We can renew the way that communities and citizenship work. Leadership, the power of small groups, the ability to fulfill a mayor's vision using technology, the use of analytic capacity across agencies to solve big problems in advance and focus the resources of previously mechanistic government agencies: the virtuous cycle potential of these elements and tools brings us closer than we have ever been in the past to the ideal of responsive government.

As we tie together these threads of empowerment, engagement, and enablement, we have two more stories to relate. For the first, we return to Indiana—this time to explore an extensive experiment aimed at reducing infant mortality and launching a statewide data analytics center. For the second, we return to New York City, this time to examine its beefed-up 311 system. Both of these stories are about pushing the envelope of data use, because they suggest that data from many sources, including highly personal information about individual citizens, will ultimately be stored and accessed in an entirely fluid and free-form fashion. Ungoverned, that kind of storage may pose risks to the fabric of democracy that we are trying to strengthen. We will need to think hard about how best to liberate civic authorities to use data well while also denying them too much data-fueled power over citizens' lives.

That is where leadership, once more, will be needed. It will take true leaders to overcome all the obstacles now in the way of relatively primitive data sharing and collaboration; it will also take leaders to ensure that we remain aware and thoughtful about potential unintended consequences of a future in which these systems are capable of far more sophisticated uses.

The Promise of Data Analytics: Indiana

In the Introduction, we briefly introduced Paul Baltzell, who took up the issue of child mortality when he became Indiana's chief information officer in January 2013. A thoughtful, straight-shooting techie with three children whom he describes as the center of his world, Baltzell is passionate about the issue: Indiana's infant mortality rate is higher than that of nearly all other US states. In his comfortable midwestern twang, he describes how digital technology should be used to save lives. Today, thanks to the work of Judge Jim Payne, whom we also described in the Introduction, an Indiana caseworker can access information on a tablet about a particular mother and child. Baltzell wants to do more: he wants that tablet to provide predictive analytics to help the caseworker make the right decisions on the spot.

It's already known that uncertain access to health care, poor nutrition, and unsafe sleeping environments contribute to infant and child deaths. But other government data—from family and health agencies, finance agencies, or business and employment agencies—may offer details about a family that correlate with risk of harm to a child. What if the fieldworker could have access to predictions about the likelihood of future harm based on a real-time analysis of these predictive factors? Casting a wider net for government data that may be relevant, Baltzell notes, "We may find connections that we didn't know existed."

Baltzell's program is also helping his staff to connect their work to the community, which embodies one of the themes of this book. He is empowering his IT employees, who are thrilled that they can help kids rather than simply run servers. "IT guys, we help people, but it's just with their computer usually," Baltzell says. On this project, though, his people "feel like they're changing the world."

Hunting for predictors of family dysfunction may not sound like the job description of a government CIO, but in fact, Baltzell notes, he's well positioned to make this analytic project a reality. "It's much easier for us to make [data-sharing] deals with agencies," he says, "because we already have relationships in place with each of them."

If the work succeeds as he envisions it, a future Indiana child services caseworker will have both personal data—information about the parents and child, contact information for other social service workers involved with the family, and any appropriate history—plus analytics that estimate the effect of various family risk factors, all on a tablet screen. For example, he says, the worker could see that "dad's on parole, mom's got a substance abuse problem, and they're receiving benefits from this agency, but maybe they're missing out on this other benefit. And, by the way, there have been three other reported incidents that correlate to more problems." Real-time data crunching would relate the family's case to analysis based on all at-risk families. The result would be a risk estimate, stated in clear terms. It might, for example, report that "this child has an 80 percent chance of something really bad happening," Baltzell says. "You need to remove him right now." Of course, most cases lack that clarity, but that's exactly the reason analytics are useful. The algorithm might report, for instance, a slight but real chance that something bad can happen—say, 10 percent—but that contacting the right parole officer could eliminate that risk.

Of course, as they use the analytics, workers will also be contributing more information to the system, adding data and helping to refine how it is used. "We will start with a small subset and then gradually add data as we determine what is truly pertinent and helpful," Baltzell says. "By doing it in this gradual fashion, we believe we'll maximize our ability to deliver good-quality, secure data and have a lot of small successes lead to the larger overall win," reducing the number of infant and child deaths in Indiana.

Baltzell's work-in-progress exemplifies how a digital approach can amplify results. First, it's a big idea: pool all government data available, and analyze what you have gathered to better target interventions. Second, the use case of reducing infant mortality is so compelling that it overrides agency sharing recalcitrance. Third, the work is being done by a collaboration of dedicated people whose job descriptions, under traditional approaches to government, would never have connected them to the issue. (In this case, Baltzell is involving researchers from Indiana University, which runs the state's backup disaster recovery data center, as well as academics and data scientists from Purdue and Ball State.)

Fourth, the project will have a ripple effect on government well beyond its immediate impact on constituents in Indiana.

According to a 2011 report by McKinsey & Company, the United States alone faces a shortage of 140,000 to 190,000 people with analytical expertise by 2018 as well as a shortage of 1.5 million managers who have the skills to understand and make decisions based on data analyses.[1] Thanks to Baltzell's project, which provides clinical opportunities for Purdue's aspiring data scientists, Indiana stands to benefit from a larger pool of well-trained graduates. With more data scientists available, more private sector businesses will be able to sell data services. That means economic growth in Indiana.

Baltzell does possess a distinct advantage in that his department already hosts all of the state government's data. "We're more of a centralized model, like a corporation would be," Baltzell says. Then, too, the state has another crucial trait: leadership from the top. "Governor [Mike] Pence is in on this," Baltzell notes. "He gives a fantastic speech talking about *Moneyball*," Michael Lewis's book on the data revolution in baseball. "He gets where data analytics is going."[2] At the same time, Baltzell's project also illustrates the profound challenges that await digital approaches to governance, to which its advocates must pay heed. He and his team have to resolve a host of questions before the first caseworker sees a new app that will help her act with discretion and professionalism. Will the public trust that data about them is being used appropriately? Will agencies share their data, or will they feel threatened and obstruct the flow of information? Will individual government workers feel empowered by connectedness and data sharing, or will the always-on communication of their tablets make them feel they have lost their autonomy?

The fact that Baltzell's project focuses on infant mortality has helped quiet the doubters. Everyone wants to save children. Nonetheless, he too runs into the kind of resistance we've seen in earlier chapters. As his department brought in a vendor to work on this single use case, Baltzell "started to see people going, 'Yeah, we're a little nervous about sharing the data.'" These people did not sit atop the agencies but rather were lifetime civil servants working at the middle levels of government who had developed a particular approach to their work over many years. Not all of their hesitation was cultural. Some told the team that sharing their data would violate federal regulations. Baltzell doesn't specify which laws or regulations. The details change with the agencies involved. But the objection keeps coming up.

Baltzell has a healthy respect for the substantial privacy concerns that agencies have. Like Linda Gibbs, he says legal standards are routinely overinterpreted by government lawyers. And federal rules on sharing information in some areas—education, for one—are unclear. But Baltzell still hasn't brought education data into his project.

Other agencies, meanwhile, are worried about the security of their data. Baltzell reports that his centralized data center manages operating systems and databases, but the applications used to extract the data are often under the control of individual agencies, as is usually the case when an application is used only by one agency. Although Baltzell's office already hosts all of their data, the agencies felt there was a risk that the infant mortality project would somehow put their data into the wrong hands.

He had an answer for that. Using security measures, his team will wall off the big data portion of the operation from the rest of Indiana's data center. The analytics operation—where particular datasets from different agencies are combined so algorithms can be run to look for patterns—will be entirely separate from the environment in which agencies store their data. In fact, the analytics area won't even be connected to the Internet. The data center has firewalls keeping the rest of the world out and already has protected areas for tax-related data; now it has "another layer of the onion" keeping "big data away from everybody else here," Baltzell says.

All the mathematical algorithms that chew through this data—the questions asked of the data in order to see whether correlations or patterns are revealed—will be handled by the Office of Technology. Employees of that department will be using packages of algorithms, subject to checks and balances created by an elaborate change management system that includes approval by several managers and two technical approvers. They will then go into a secure, access-controlled room in order to run those algorithms with the help of new software tools that work through data still sitting in temporary computer memory—allowing real-time processing and therefore enabling decisions based on this data to be made much more quickly than with normal analytical tools.

To limit abuse, these select employees won't be able to download data, and accountability will be maintained through the system's forensic ability to report who accessed the data and for what reason. The data scientists and students involved with developing those algorithms will be given access to only what they need.

The data fed into the system from the agencies will be earmarked to make clear that it's authorized for use only in particular, highly defined circumstances; any extensions of those use cases will themselves be subject to a carefully defined process. Asking questions of the data, like the hosting of the data, will be the subject of a clear set of authorization rules. The plan is for the benefits of data analytics to cascade throughout the organization, with different employees at different levels asking important "What if?" questions. But each will have access only to appropriately limited data.

Another advantage of a consolidated dataset for government is that information can be analyzed to assess the performance of the agencies that use it. The Office of Technology will be able to support agencies in their efforts to improve their selection of key performance indicators. (The idea is to move from indicators that measure too many inputs or activities to those that measure outcomes.) This new approach to data will also enhance agencies' ability to report quickly about compound issues—money spent per problem, ratio of employees to constituents served—that can then be filled in with hard information rather than anecdote. The new term for this function, he says, will be the "Management and Performance Hub," or MPH. (As Baltzell puts it, "In government, we absolutely love acronyms. If there isn't one, we feel like we have to create one.") The idea of a thoroughly integrated data-informed public performance management system is still relatively new, and Baltzell is determined that Indiana will be a leader in this area. Under its previous governor, Mitch Daniels, Indiana drove the performance of its agencies relentlessly; what Baltzell provides his new boss, Governor Pence, is the ability to use real-time, outcome-based metrics bolstered by far greater access to data.

Baltzell, though, understands that he needs to work with many people beyond just his boss. He must get the career civil servants within the state agencies on board. (That, by the way, is one more reason he's eager to work through their legal concerns rather than resolve them with an executive order mandating cooperation.) "Because when the rubber meets the road, even if the agency head's on board, and they're telling him to do it, you need them to share their business knowledge," he says of agency staff. "No matter what data you collect, you really need the business owners who understand the data and where they came from." To design algorithms that chew through many databases to find patterns, he knows, the data team needs the collective wisdom of the civil servants.

Big issues still face Baltzell's team as it works toward its goal. When is information sufficient to improve decision making? The team will need to avoid making the perfect (use of all possible data) be the enemy of the good enough (use of enough data to power a vast improvement over the status quo). With caseworkers responsible for children's lives, the consequences of a flaw—say, inaccurate data or a faulty algorithm that leads a caseworker to wrongly decide whether to remove a child from her family home—are as severe as they come. And when, as is inevitable in any human enterprise, flaws are discovered, how will the agency defend general improvement against the claims of the single anecdote? In the highly charged world of child welfare, after results improve for nine children from the analytics effort, the department still must be prepared to be on the defensive for the one with the worse result.

Workers, not machines, will be making the decisions about child welfare; Baltzell's vision is that data-informed ("smarter") workers will make better decisions more frequently. The team will need to have benchmarks in place from the beginning that are capable of reliably measuring and demonstrating improvement; zero defects, after all, is an impossible goal in this very human context.

On this issue, it's important to recognize that bureaucrats are not the only people whose assumptions are challenged by digital governance. The public, too, has a set of assumptions about "normal" government, and data-driven approaches will disrupt it. Personalized services for citizens will help the vast number of families who apply for benefits, and those applicants are already used to answering questions about their incomes. But what about the person who has an outstanding tax warrant that shows up in a data search when he or she applies for a state contract?

Already, big data projects, both commercial and governmental, have drawn complaints. Baltzell distinguishes beneficial government information hubs from invasive tracking: "With the NSA and [Edward] Snowden, a lot of the public has the misperception that any government entity performing data analytics is trying to watch them, and that's not what we're doing. We're just using historical data, things that happened to children, and applying it to present-day cases, hoping to improve outcomes."

Ignoring the trade-offs from personalized and analyzed data will only raise risks. To some extent, citizens already provide sensitive information to their government, including when they file taxes or apply for means-tested benefits of a customized government. Many will appreciate opportunities to sign up for information programs whose benefit they immediately understand, like automatically generated and neighborhood-specific city messages. And many will understand that a system should be able to determine which applicants for benefits have broken the law in some way in order to give them a second look and that public workers with access to more information and better training will make better decisions. But there are real issues triggered by the broad use of data that will need careful policy work, even if the overall quality of citizens' lives and the responsiveness of their government are improved through data-driven governance.

These are the areas where good communication and official self-restraint are going to be essential. A governor who is "all in"—like Indiana's Mike Pence—can help the public understand oversight mechanisms and constraints on the use of information. He can be open about the incremental, careful nature of his government's approach to data and the powerful oversight measures he has put in place to reduce as much as possible the risk of abuse. To have that dialogue, he is going to need to first have his team develop thoughtful policy, in consultation with civil society representatives and the public, that sets the parameters for what his employees can do. In fact, Pence and Baltzell started very deliberately paying attention to privacy and security first.

Another theme of this book is the great power of digital governance to increase civic participation and trust in government. But data-driven approaches must retain the confidence of the public. Without that, digital governance risks entrenching and amplifying the deficit of public trust that has existed for decades.

In sum, as we have noted often in these pages, leadership matters. It is up to public leaders to define how data should be treated and secured—and then to carefully explain how long-term benefits outweigh short-term fears.

The Promise of 311: New York City

New York City's is another government that is thinking big when it comes to the digital revolution. NYC.gov, the entry point into all New York City information, gets thirty-five million hits every year—close to eighty thousand a day. During Hurricane Irene in August 2011, constituents were using NYC.gov to get reliable information about the effects of the massive storm and to watch live feeds of the mayor's broadcasts. The site almost buckled under the strain. It had not been an optimal public face for the city in the first place; its user interface was clunky and its back end was not easily extended to take in additional data. "If we wanted to change the content of the site in real time, it was just not possible," recalls Rahul Merchant, New York City's first chief information and innovation officer reporting directly to the mayor, who served in the Bloomberg administration from 2012 to 2013.

Merchant and his team wanted to make NYC.gov the most scalable, most useful, user-friendly, and social media–friendly site possible. He wanted it to hook into New York City's 311 system. And he wanted to make 311, in turn, the overlay, for internal New York City government purposes, of all city data. The first step of that plan is done. In less than seventeen months, NYC.gov was rebuilt with a content management system that is scalable and has hooks into every city agency as well as the 311 system. Merchant is proud: he thinks this site can interface with many more agencies than healthcare.gov does and for far less money. "This is not just for health insurance," he says. "This is for everything. It is like the lifeblood of the city."

Like so many others we have profiled in this book, Merchant believes his achievements are only a beginning and that much greater things lie ahead. For instance, he says, the city's 311 system is going to become the largest customer management system on the planet.

After the big hurricane that followed Irene—Sandy, the deadliest and most destructive hurricane of 2012, and the second costliest in US history—New York City wanted citizens to be able to apply for cheap loans or rapid repair programs. But to add that capability to the old 311 system took months, and even after the system was up, it wasn't able to tell the city if any particular applicant had applied to other city programs as well.

That will soon be a problem of the past. Once the planned upgrade of the city's systems is complete, Merchant says, each constituent and each building in the city could be assigned a unique identifier that could allow them to be tracked through all parts of government. New York City, like Amazon or Netflix, will know with whom it is dealing at every digital encounter. That will let the city personalize its responses to each constituent. And the New York City government will be able to target its interactions. A resident will no longer need to call each week to ask whether she needs to move her car because of alternate side-of-the-street parking rules. Instead, she will be able to register with the system and ask for a notice to be sent automatically to her. Government on her terms, not its.

The city's system will allow constituents to reach any agency through NYC.gov—itself an approachable layer over the city's 311 system. That 311 system in turn rests on top of the data operations of all city agencies. In other words, New York City's residents will have easy access to an immense trove of information about their city.

Technology breakthroughs, particularly those involving large projects like 311, face another substantial problem: retaining sought-after, well-paid management capable of protecting the city's interest as it manages a complex ecosystem of outside vendors. Public salaries in these competitive areas are traditionally well below those of the private sector. But for cities to get the most out of their contractors, they must be able to use high-quality project management talent.

To get this 311 upgrade done, Merchant employed a novel approach to city project management. He found an exceptionally talented city employee who was a project manager within the

Department of Information Technology and Telecommunications and had her hired by the New York City Technology Development Corporation (TDC), a nonprofit and very lean consulting organization that has only one client: the City of New York. This transfer allowed the employee to be retained with a 20 percent pay increase that closed some of the gap between what the city and the private sector could pay. More important, the employee was empowered to enforce decision making and coordination across city agencies and vendors alike. With help from the Mayor's office and Deputy Mayor Cas Holloway (whom we met in chapter 6), she had the authority to bang heads among the other agencies. That newly minted project manager insisted on extensive testing and careful timelines for design changes. (These are both safeguards that, Merchant points out, were not present for the deeply flawed launch of the federal healthcare.gov project.)

Merchant is proud of the TDC idea. He believes this is the first time this approach has been brought to bear on the problem all cities have with project management. Getting top talent to focus—at low cost—on systems that need cross-agency coordination is always hard, but the outside-consultant approach is working.

In fact, the New York City 311 story weaves together several themes we have explored in this book. It's clearly important to find a way to manage projects that takes advantage of employees' skills and empowers them to act as professionals with authority to get the job done across multiple agencies. It's obvious too that government's engagement with its residents will be better by knowing more about the health of its city services. Making 311 the unifying platform for city data ties those services to what constituents actually care about. Soon citizens will be able to comment on 311 data through their smartphones. That fosters the connection between government and its citizens that so many constituents yearn for. If all goes well, New York's 311 will finally become a platform for civic engagement rather than a database of complaints. And the availability of such vast stores of public data for reuse, research, and visualization will enable citizens to work with local government on shared solutions to the big problems that cities face.

All told, with a system of unique and persistent identifiers for constituents and buildings, plus social media sensing (enhancing official information with data supplied by residents in real time) and the use of 311 as an internal city platform to connect requests to metrics, New York City's government will be transformed. It will know and understand its residents and their interactions with its services in a much deeper way than it ever did before. The result: an enormous reservoir of data from many sources, accessible to many people, making possible the codevelopment of solutions to urban challenges. As Merchant puts it, "It's all one thing. This city is going to be a different place."

Private Data Publicly Used: The Need for Thoughtful Public Policy

This sounds like breathtaking progress and possibility; it's just the kind of development this book celebrates. At the same time, New York City, like Indiana, will have to reckon with the important public policies that should govern the use of such a vast amount of data—how access to data will be overseen and constrained, what programs citizens will be opting into, how long information will be retained, how abuses will be punished, how information will be effectively anonymized, and many other issues.

Consider the case of responsive environments—places where sensors are embedded in many locations, and even in everyday objects, in order to better monitor and understand people's behavior in those places. In February 2014, the *New York Times* published a piece on the subject. It described how LED light fixtures at Newark Airport are now part of a network of sensors and cameras that collect data.[3] It's a useful system: the patterns emerging from this data can be used to "spot long lines, recognize license plates and even identify suspicious activity," according to reporter Diane Cardwell. The companies building and selling these systems to public authorities are excited: they see whole new markets built out of mundane functions (like lighting).

What happens in airports can happen on city streets, as we have described in this book. Streetlamps, for example, can have networked sensors that make them part of systems that control traffic, check for environmental hazards, notice when garbage cans are full, listen for gunshots, watch for security breaches, find parking places, issue security alerts, and more. With the Internet of Things—where sensors like these connect—officials will be able to monitor and anticipate system changes. This ability will continue to increase as the sophistication of sensors rises and the costs decrease.

But data that can be used can also be misused. Professor Fred Cate, director of the Center for Applied Cybersecurity Research at Indiana University, told Cardwell that the potential for misuse of the gathered data was "terrifying." A problem with big data technology, he believes, is that in some sense, it is too easy to use. Rather than giving careful thought to the types of information a system needs, users find it easier to just vacuum up everything. And then, having stored it, they may not give enough thought to the problem of managing it.

The potential for trouble is obvious. Sensors are getting cheaper, and city governments, for all the reasons we have outlined in this book, are increasingly eager to gather all the data they can on their operations. Yet the policy backbone that should guide data collection, aggregation, and use by city agencies does not exist in most places.

If the digital revolution is to succeed and bring about a new birth of civic life, we will need to ensure that city governments develop the capacity to use data with good judgment. And we hasten to add that much of the benefit of data mining can come from the use of anonymous data or data the resident affirmatively allows the city to use. After all, there is clearly value to all of this digital information and its ability to melt bureaucracy—forcing it, in effect, to go through a phase change that we hope will result in increased democratic responsiveness. Because the data analytics effort is new and relatively immature, this is the right time to carry out the tough work of dealing with the privacy implications of a more responsive city.

The process of collection is not going to stop. We think, in fact, that it would be shortsighted and probably impossible to halt this natural evolution. That is all the more reason, then, to carefully establish policies covering data access, data security, and transparency with respect to its collection. Forensic capacity—to look back and see who had access to what for what reason—should be a top priority in the development of any data system. So should clear consequences for data misuse by government employees. These safeguards are essential if the public is to develop confidence that government data tools work for its betterment, not against it.

Above all, we think it is important that these new developments be understood as tools, not as ends in themselves. The ultimate purpose of this digital revolution in governance should be to make life more worth living. The progressive reforms of the nineteenth century began with good intentions, but then they sank under a heavy weight of process. Rather than existing for the reasons the reformers stated, many aspects of government exist because they exist, and too bad if they suffocate ingenuity. Responsive digital governance must avoid this tendency to create institutions without justification.

We must not embrace the use of digital tools for its own sake. Instead, our shared goal should be to thicken the bonds of democracy in our cities by making them more responsive. Not everyone will agree about which uses of data are nurturing and which uses are intrusive or dehumanizing.

This tension will be with us for a long time, and we will need a great deal of respectful conversation to resolve it. Fortunately (to return to another theme of this book) digital tools make communication astonishingly easy. At this crucial moment in the development of urban policy, we need to make the most of these opportunities for conversation about how to preserve primary human values as we change the tools of government. We must have a sophisticated consensus about how to move through this digital revolution while maintaining human dignity and autonomy for both government workers and citizens.

Employed in the service of a more responsive urban environment, data-smart efforts can spur renewal of civic pride and engagement. As Children's Optimal Health, the nonprofit data aggregator we profiled in chapter 2, discovered in Austin, looking at data on a shared screen can limit kneejerk emotional responses to difficult policy questions while encouraging everyone involved to focus on real problems and work together. When data tools let people see the facts and trend lines attached to an issue, they are less tempted to tussle over old slights and imagined injuries. Reliable information, presented understandably, can even promote empathy. As Linda Gibbs imagines, government employees with access to a data picture of a constituent's life can be more understanding of the context of that person's behavior. That's a perspective they can use to intervene more effectively.

The humanizing power of visualized information—its ability to calm people and foster cooperation—must be kept in mind as the digital governance revolution progresses. If data is employed in an automatic, disassociated way, creating decision rules that ignore context and human agency, then these new tools will amplify public skepticism about the role of government. That would undermine the heroic work of the people we have profiled in this book. If we could talk to the generation of leaders that earnestly put in place the progressive reforms aimed at cleaning up the corruption of early twentieth-century local government, we would say: make sure you periodically evaluate whether the rules are actually serving key public values. Be willing to reverse or moderate your course as needed. Focus on problem solving rather than rule following. We believe today's leaders should have that kind of self-awareness as they create the data-driven, responsive governments of this century.

We are confident they can and that their vision of a better civic life can be achieved. And, of course, we believe they will get there even more quickly if they follow our parting advice.

First, they should push their governments to see problems as horizontal rather than vertical issues. Today, agencies still see data as turf to be defended. Part of the reason is mechanical: ancient systems—only slightly newer than the typewriters Bill Oates encountered when he showed up in Boston City Hall—do not allow interoperability across agency barriers. Employees in different departments do redundant, overlapping work. Attempts to break them out of their seclusion can be stymied by overly cautious readings of relevant statutes. All the government energy now devoted to self-protection needs to be redirected. It needs to flow instead into collaboration, joint problem solving, and professional approaches. That will require not just a vision of a better government but the leadership to make that vision a reality.

Second, digital advocates should collaborate with ordinary citizens as much as possible. Far too little of Americans' growing data savvy is aimed at solving civic problems. Willing and able people who want to use technology to make life better for their communities are out there. Government needs to connect with them. At the most basic level, cities need to ensure that citizens have world-class Internet access at reasonable prices. Cities are now platforms, and it is crucial for economic development and civic life that everyone be wired. Of course, citizens must be deeply involved in decisions about the deployment of data technology. New kinds of sensors—part of streetlights or software that analyzes tweets—can help create better policies. But that can't happen unless the people monitored by those sensors have something to say about their deployment. Finally, outreach to citizens shouldn't be limited to individuals. Fixing procurement processes would allow small local businesses to provide solutions to local problems in cost-effective ways.

Third, the digital revolutionaries in city government should look hard for ways to free their employees to act with discretion and professionalism. Apps that permit employees to see context as well as detail; job descriptions that empower civil servants to take risks and learn new subjects; hiring practices that take into account real-world experience and encourage easy entry by technology-adept, entrepreneurial employees: all of these should be in the toolbox of urban leaders. So should the digital tools that let government track more quickly and accurately exactly what its employees are doing. As we have described in earlier chapters, mobile data and communications technology can expand both worker discretion and worker accountability.

On this point, we are particularly excited about the pipeline of millennials going into public service. Younger millennials are now students or recent graduates, and they will use their comfort with digital technology and social media for the public good. These young people are demanding training and opportunities at the intersection of technology, policy, and governance. They are dissatisfied with governments that don't serve their citizens' needs well and irritated at the disconnect between citizens and their government. They will be the ones who will bridge the gap between their lived experience in the digital world and the current reality of civic life. At home with digital technology, they see clearly how it can transform government operations. They understand how much the thoughtful use of technology can improve urban life and the business of government.

The millennials grasp that digital technology can quickly gather the best ideas, bring people together to look at a shared problem, and create a quick response that then is fed back into the discussion. They see that such processes allow all participants to be more creative in finding solutions while using fewer resources. Local governments need to be restructured so as to take advantage of this generation's skills. A good start would be for government to separate out traditional IT functions (keeping the servers running, setting up e-mail systems), outsource them where possible, and let its young tech-savvy employees focus more on technology's role in policymaking.

As we remarked at the start of this book, we are at a turning point in the history of governance—another watershed of the same proportions as Progressive government over a century ago. The advent of electricity made it possible for government agencies to be far more productive. The introduction of the telephone made sharing information far easier. Today data and technology are recreating those revolutions, but at a rate and on a scale that are difficult for human minds to grasp. The new technology has improved the effectiveness and efficiency of legacy processes, as we've mentioned. But the real payoff will come when technology changes legacy processes for good to create truly data-smart and responsive cities.

The stories told in the preceding pages illustrate how cities can empower, engage, and enable both public employees and citizens. Enhanced by digital technology, these cities will change the way citizens view local government and civic life itself. But this revolution, like any other, needs to respect its inheritance and preserve the strengths of earlier forms of urban government: human leadership and judgment. After all, this digital revolution is not being fought for the sake of apps and tablets. It will succeed, and transform civic life for the better, by making it once again of the people, for the people, and by the people.

Notes

Introduction

1. Stephen Goldsmith, "Progressive Government Is Obsolete," *Wall Street Journal*, March 18, 2011.
2. Anne Marie Warren, Ainin Sulaiman, and Noor Ismawati Jaafar, "Social Media Effects on Fostering Online Civic Engagement and Building Citizen Trust and Trust in Institutions," *Government Information Quarterly* (in press).
3. Shari Hyman, "Enforcement and Data: One New York City Agency's Vision for a Level Playing Field," *Data-Smart City Solutions*, August 13, 2013.

Chapter 1

1. Andrew Ryan, "Mayor Menino Widely Backed, But Another Run Isn't," *Boston Globe*, March 27, 2013.
2. Shannon Bond, "Northeast Hit by Severe Winter Weather," *US Society*, January 4, 2014.
3. Katharine Q. Seelye, "Two Decades of Change Have Boston Sparkling," *New York Times*, January 5, 2014.
4. Michael Levenson, "The New Urban Mechanic Mayor Moves On," *Boston Globe*, March 28, 2013.
5. Donovan Slack, "City Complaint Line Lags," *Boston Globe*, April 6, 2008.
6. Donovan Slack, "Computer System Quickens City Response to Complaints," *Boston Globe*, May 27, 2009.
7. Alex Pentland, *Social Physics* (New York: Penguin Press, 2014), p. 65.

Chapter 2

1. Julie Zauzmer, "Mayor Gray Celebrates DC's Good Grades," *Washington Post,* July 9, 2013.
2. Adrien Schless-Meier, "K[no]w Vacancy: From NY to PA, Urban Land Maps Support Reclaiming Abandoned Lots," *Civil Eats,* July 26, 2013.
3. Jasper Hamill, "Could Google Maps End Poverty?" *Forbes,* January 28, 2014.

Chapter 3

1. "Mayor Bloomberg Announces Winners of NYC Bigapps, Fourth Annual Competition to Create Apps Using City Data," press release, NYC.gov, June 20, 2013.
2. Vincent Homburg, *Understanding E-Government: Information Systems in Public Administration* (New York: Routledge, 2008).
3. Albert O. Hirschman, *Exit, Voice, and Loyalty: Responses to Decline in Firms, Organizations, and States* (Cambridge, MA: Harvard University Press, 1970).
4. Knight Soul of the Community, "Why People Love Where They Live and Why It Matters: A National Perspective" (2010), www.soulofthecommunity.org.
5. Margreet Frieling, Siegwart Lindenberg, and Frans Stokman, "Collaborative Communities through Coproduction: Two Case Studies," *American Review of Public Administration* 44 (2014): 35–58.
6. Ray Forrest and Ade Kearns, "Social Cohesion, Social Capital and the Neighbourhood," *Urban Studies* 38 (2001): 2125–43.
7. Nicco Mele, *The End of Big: How the Internet Makes David the New Goliath* (New York: St. Martin's Press, 2013).
8. Julie Zauzmer, "Mayor Gray Celebrates DC's Good Grades," *Washington Post,* July 9, 2013.
9. Alfred Tat-Kei Ho, "Reinventing Local Government and the e-Government Initiative," *Public Administration Review* 62 (2002): 434–44.

Chapter 4

1. John Pletz, "Tech Chief Tolva Leaving City Hall," *Crain's Chicago Business,* October 22, 2013.
2. Karen Mossberger, Caroline Tolbert, and Chris Anderson, "Measuring Change in Internet Use and Broadband Adoption: Comparing BTOP Smart Communities and Other Chicago Neighborhoods," *Broadband Illinois,* February 7, 2013.
3. Ibid.
4. "New City Crime Database Goes Online," *Chicago Tribune,* September 14, 2011.
5. Robert Scoble and Shel Israel, *Age of Context* (Patrick Brewster Press, 2014).

Chapter 5

1. David E. Bowen and Edward E. Lawler, "The Empowerment of Service Workers: What, Why, How, and When," *Sloan Management Review* 333 (1992): 31–39.
2. Alan A. Altshuler and Robert D. Behn, *Innovation in American Government: Challenges, Opportunities, and Dilemmas* (Washington, DC: Brookings Institution, 1997).
3. Michael Lipsky, *Street-Level Bureaucracy: Dilemmas of the Individual in Public Service,* 30th anniversary expanded ed. (New York: Russell Sage Foundation, 2010).
4. Ibid.
5. Sergio Fernandez and Tima Moldogaziev, "Employee Empowerment, Employee Attitudes, and Performance: Testing a Causal Model," *Public Administration Review* 73 (2013): 490–506.

Chapter 7

1. Michael Barbaro, "Bloomberg Focuses on Rest (as in Rest of the World)," *New York Times,* December 14, 2013.
2. Zachary Tumin, "New York's HHS-Connect: IT Crosses Boundaries in a Shared-MissionWorld," *Governing.com,* August 24, 2009.

3. Steven Greenhouse, "City to Press for Easing of Civil Service Requirements," *New York Times,* January 6, 2011.
4. Sarah Rich, "Boosting Innovation by Rethinking Government Procurement," *Government Technology,* October 28, 2013.
5. Clay Johnson, "Seven Simple Ways to Modernize Enterprise Procurement" (Atlanta, GA: Department of Better Technology, 2013), http://www. dobt.co.

Chapter 8

1. James Manyika and others, "Big Data: The Next Frontier for Innovation, Competition, and Productivity" (McKinsey Global Institute, May 2011).
2. Mike Pence, address to Indiana Digital Government Summit, October 24, 2013.
3. Diane Cardwell, "At Newark Airport, the Lights Are On, and They're Watching You," *New York Times,* February 17, 2014.

Acknowledgments

We express our appreciation to the many people who assisted us with this book. The work leading to it was supported by Bloomberg Philanthropies, which has funded our Data-Smart City Solutions project. In particular, our thanks go to Patricia Harris and James Anderson and, of course, to Michael Bloomberg himself, whose business and government leadership have provided proof of many of the theories advocated in this book. These individuals supported work on digital governance reforms before these issues gained the widespread attention they now receive. Our work on digital responsiveness has also been supported by Alaina Harkness of the John D. and Catherine T. MacArthur Foundation, a key leader in the international movement; Carol Coletta of the John S. and James L. Knight Foundation; Mark Steinmeyer of the Smith Richardson Foundation; and Jenny Toomey of the Ford Foundation. We also have enjoyed the important support of the Inter-American Development Bank and the National League of Cities.

Many individuals at Harvard's Kennedy School of Government and Harvard Law School have been instrumental in making this book possible. In particular, we recognize the enormously important, ongoing, and diligent support of key staff at the Ash Center for Democratic Governance and Innovation at Harvard Kennedy School, including the work of Kara O'Sullivan, Katherine Hillenbrand, Jessica Casey, Matthew McClellan, Alicia Gessell, and Sean Thornton. Each of these people helps us advocate for more effective governance through digital tools every day. Marty Mauzy, executive director of the Ash Center, and Christina Marchand, who manages the Innovations in American Government Award program, also played important roles. Many of our theories about enlightened public sector principles have been influenced by the crucial work of Mark Moore, our colleague at Harvard.

Furthermore, we benefit from our students and research assistants, all of whom helped with research, blogging, and drafting. In particular, we thank and acknowledge Benjamin Weinryb Grohsgal, Needham Hurst, Dana Walters, Andrew Glantz, and Melissa Nally.

We appreciate the guidance of Alison Hankey and her associates at Jossey-Bass who helped us produce this book. In addition, Alina Gorokhovsky, a corporate strategist who supports our work with our partner Living Cities, assisted in the identification and analysis of some of the cases about which we wrote. Portions of this work have been adapted from content originally published by Governing.com, Data-Smart City Solutions, the Berkman Center for Internet & Society, the Roosevelt Institute, and the Manhattan Institute. Our work with these organizations has helped us refine our thinking about responsive government.

Finally, we are indebted to the pioneering public servants featured in this book, who are leading the way toward a new era of government.

About the Authors

Stephen Goldsmith is the Daniel Paul Professor of the Practice of Government and director of the Innovations in Government Program at Harvard's Kennedy School of Government. He is a nationally recognized expert on government management, reform, and innovation. Goldsmith currently directs Data-Smart City Solutions, a project to highlight local government efforts to use new technologies that connect breakthroughs in the use of big data analytics with community input to reshape the relationship between government and citizen.

Goldsmith previously served as deputy mayor of New York and mayor of Indianapolis, where he earned a reputation as one of the country's leaders in public-private partnerships, competition, and privatization. He was also the chief domestic policy advisor to the George W. Bush campaign in 2000, the chair of the Corporation for National and Community Service, and the district attorney for Marion County, Indiana, from 1979 to 1990.

Goldsmith has written *The Power of Social Innovation*; *Governing by Network: The New Shape of the Public Sector*; *Putting Faith in Neighborhoods: Making Cities Work through Grassroots Citizenship*; and *The Twenty-First Century City: Resurrecting Urban America*. His columns have frequently been published in such newspapers as the *Wall Street Journal* and the *New York Times*. Goldsmith is a graduate of Wabash College and the University of Michigan Law School.

. . . .

Susan Crawford is the John A. Reilly Visiting Professor in Intellectual Property at the Harvard Law School. She is a professor at the Benjamin N. Cardozo School of Law, a fellow at the

Roosevelt Institute, and a codirector of the Berkman Center. She is the author of *Captive Audience: The Telecom Industry and Monopoly Power in the New Gilded Age* and a contributor to *Bloomberg View* and *Wired*. She served as special assistant to the president for science, technology, and innovation policy (2009) and co-led the Federal Communications Commission transition team between the Bush and Obama administrations. She also served as a member of Mayor Michael Bloomberg's Advisory Council on Technology and Innovation.

Crawford was formerly a visiting Stanton Professor of the First Amendment at Harvard Kennedy School, a visiting professor at Harvard Law School, and a professor at the University of Michigan Law School (2008–2010). She was a member of the board of directors of ICANN from 2005 to 2008.

Crawford received her BA and JD from Yale University. She served as a clerk for Judge Raymond J. Dearie of the US District Court for the Eastern District of New York and was a partner at Wilmer, Cutler & Pickering (now WilmerHale).

Index

"Gotcha!" world, 58, 101
Governing magazine, 154
Grade.DC.gov, 37–38, 68
Gray, Vincent, 38
GreenThumb, 46
Grounded, 46
Groups, psychology of, 54

H
Hamilton, Ulla, 154
Harkness, Alaina, 42
Harrington, Patrick, 25
Harvard Business School, 24, 29
Harvard Kennedy School, 2, 98, 105
Harvard University, 2, 14, 42
Health, Department of (DOH), 11, 130
Health and Hospitals Corporation, 146
Health and human services, 140. *See also* HHS-Connect
Health and Mental Hygiene, Department of, 140
Healthcare.gov, 36, 151, 169, 171
Heat islands, using sensors to address, 77
Heat maps, 48, 101
Heeke, Stefan, 101
Helping Hands, 56
HHS-Connect, 140–147
Hierarchies: command-and-control barriers of, difficulty removing, 113; flattening, 102; leadership from the top essential to replacing, 15; by-product of, 112–113; replacing rigid, 157; social media upending, 14
High-speed Internet access: citizens organizing for, 43; city improving, 73, 74–76, 77
Hiring, 111, 148, 149, 176
Hirschman, Albert O., 59
Hirst, Martha K., 149
Ho, Alfred Tat-Kei, 69
Holloway, Cas, 134–135, 171
Holmes, Justin, 26, 28, 149, 150
Holtzman, Elizabeth, 105
Homburg, Vincent, 57

Homeless Services, Department of, 101–102, 140
Horizontal organization, 6, 175
Horn, Martin, 141
Hotspots, identifying, 11, 48, 101
House Committee on Oversight and Government Reform, 109
Housing Authority, 106, 143
Houston School of Public Health, 48
Human resource systems, 113
Humboldt Park, 76
Hurricane Irene, 169
Hurricane Sandy, 170
Hussein, Saddam, 120, 121
Hyman, Shari, 9–11

I
IBM, 74, 84
IdeaHub, 113
Ideas: blocking the flow of, 4; free flow of, 113; sharing of, networking for, 50
Illinois, 76
Improvement: measuring and demonstrating, having benchmarks for, importance of, 167; virtuous cycle of, 32, 97, 117–118, 161
Incremental change, 160
Indian government, 51
Indiana, 7–8, 9, 147–148, 161, 162–168, 172
Indiana University, 118, 163, 173
Indianapolis, 66
Infant mortality, reducing, 9, 161
Information access, lack of, 113, 147. *See also* Data access; Real-time information, ability to access
Information flow: blocking, 4, 164; constantly changing, of 911 calls, 133; pace of, 3
Information lockdown, 142, 143
Information sharing. *See* Data sharing
Information socialization, 66
Information sources: expansion of, 3–4; reliable, notions about, liberation of cities from, 67